"Nathan Sloan brings together in ... his experience as a missionary, and his ... ng in the same local church for over a deca ... and that, as followers of Christ, we are all sent ones. ... but all professional missionaries, readers will learn what it m ... a sent follower of Christ in the ordinary rhythms of life in our comn ... es."

Jarvis J. Williams, Associate Professor of New Testament Interpretation, The Southern Baptist Theological Seminary, Louisville, KY; author of *Redemptive Kingdom Diversity* and *Christ Redeemed Us from the Curse of the Law*

"In *You Are Sent*, Nathan provides an excellent introduction to foundational ideas for every believer to consider as they pursue faithfulness to the Great Commission. This accessible work provides sufficient content for someone new to global engagement while resourcing those with some prior knowledge. I commend it to you and your ministry!"

Todd Engstrom, Executive Pastor of Ministry Strategies, The Austin Stone; cofounder, 100 UPG Cooperative

"In a straightforward, biblical, and adaptable style, Nathan Sloan provides an invaluable guidebook in preparing your church to live on mission. It will challenge everyone to consider their role in God's global mission, along with highlighting their identity as a sent one, no matter their geographic location or vocation. A must-have missions training resource."

Greg Mathias, Director of the Global Mission Center, New Orleans Baptist Theological Seminary

"*You Are Sent* is an excellent road map and resource for every church that longs to see God's people on mission yet grapples with where to start. Nathan has done a brilliant work in creating a tool that gives pastors and church leaders confidence in equipping their congregations to embrace God's heart for the nations."

Michelle Atwell, CEO, SEND US

"Nathan has a big heart for missions, and after reading this book, you will too. There are many books written on missions but few that will force you to slow down, ponder, ask questions, and try to apply it to your heart. It's a practical, accessible guide, packed with a lot of wisdom; one that should be read and paid heed to by all believers. Churches and missions pastors will do well to use this book."

Hezekiah Harshit Singh, Pastor, Satya Vachan Church, Lucknow, India

"Christ sent us to reach a big—and complicated—world. *You Are Sent* is a practical primer on that commission, written for the local church. It will help you and the people in your church understand the task of missions in a clear, biblical, and compelling way, and help lead you to your next step in completing Christ's last command."

Nate Irwin, Pastor of Global Outreach, College Park Church, Indianapolis, IN

"From biblical theology to a history of missions, and from contextualization to one's particular call to be a missionary, *You Are Sent* clearly covers all essential topics in a transferable format. More importantly, it emphasizes that God's sending of his people is not intended for a select few. Rather, wherever God has put us, we are on mission. Highly recommended!"

Gregg R. Allison, Professor of Christian Theology, The Southern Baptist Theological Seminary; secretary, Evangelical Theological Society; author of *Historical Theology* and *Sojourners and Strangers*

"Inspirational, practical, and made to order for the biggest, most diverse social network in the world: the church. Nathan's heart for the local church comes through in this book. It is combined with an equal dose of Great Commission vision. If you have been looking for a way to energize the soul of your congregation, this is the resource for you."

Ted Esler, President, Missio Nexus

"Each week in my church toward the end of the service, we pray this prayer: 'And now, Father, send us out to do the work you have given us to do, to love and serve you as faithful witnesses of Christ our Lord.' In this new work, Nathan Sloan provides tangible feet to this prayer—a practicable and reflective guide to help every believer engage in God's mission. I highly recommend it."

Edward L. Smither, Dean, College of Intercultural Studies, Columbia International University; author of *Christian Missions* and *Mission in the Early Church*

"Nathan knows God's grace and love for us is the power that propels us into our unique roles in world-wide gospel mission. As a missionary, scholar, and pastor, Nathan calls us to follow Christ into all the world with his gospel."

Josiah Bancroft, Senior Director of Mission, Serge

YOU ARE SENT

Finding Your Place in God's Global Mission

Nathan Sloan

New
Growth
Press

newgrowthpress.com

New Growth Press, Greensboro, NC 27401
newgrowthpress.com
Copyright © 2022 by Nathan Sloan

Scripture quotations are from The ESV˚ Bible (The Holy Bible, English Standard Version˚), copyright © 2001 by Crossway, a publishing ministry of Good News Publishers. Used by permission. All rights reserved.

Cover Design: Studio Gearbox
Interior Design and Typesetting: Gretchen Logterman

ISBN 978-1-64507-250-8 (Print)
ISBN 978-1-64507-251-5 (eBook)

Printed in the United States of America

29 28 27 26 25 24 23 22   1 2 3 4 5

CONTENTS

INTRODUCTION

We all want to invest our lives in something bigger than ourselves. We want to be a part of a movement and a story that matters. That's why people become die-hard sports fans, cheering on their team until they lose their voice. That's why we fall in love with stories like *The Lord of the Rings* or *Star Wars*. We long to be a part of a tribe or group fighting for a cause that has meaning far beyond our own lives.

As Christians, we are a part of the greatest story in human history: the living story of God sending his Son into our broken world to bring us back to life and into a relationship with himself. But we are more than receivers in this story. We are sent out on a mission.

A common myth in Christianity is that living on mission is just for a select few—that it takes a special calling to share Jesus and make disciples. The truth is that every Christian is called and empowered to make Jesus known. Every Christian is a part of expanding God's great kingdom. You and I are made to live sent out with the gospel.

You Are Sent is written to give you a deeper understanding and passion for global missions while at the same time equipping you to make disciples wherever you find yourself. This book will help you understand the biblical basis of mission and missions history, and then move you onward into practical ways to live on mission in your everyday life. I've written it to provide churches with a missions course that is robust in theology and missiology while at the same time being accessible to every member.

So if you are looking for a book to help you grow in your understanding of God's global mission and to equip you to live on mission in your daily life—if you long to be a part of something bigger than yourself—*You Are Sent* may be just the book you need to move out on mission with God to the world around you.

HOW TO USE THIS BOOK

This nine-week missions course has been written for use in local churches. From the very beginning, the vision has been to create a course that could be shaped and adapted based on the needs and context of your local church, whatever those are. Those who lead this course in your church have the freedom to teach *You Are Sent* in various ways, and will bring in their own experiences, thoughts, and viewpoints.

At my local church, we teach it in a classroom setting of ten to forty people for nine weeks in a row, and we encourage deeper community to happen in smaller cohorts of five to eight people. Your church may use it as a small group curriculum, for one-on-one discipleship, in a virtual teaching format, or even as a sermon series adapted for the whole church. But whichever of these your church is doing, keep in mind that *You Are Sent* is most effective when done in community with others and is not intended for you to merely study individually.

This book will walk you through the nine lessons of *You Are Sent*. These lessons will build on each other, leading you to a final lesson that will help you answer two key questions about your Christian life:

What is your role in God's global mission?

What is your next step?

You will want to have this book with you when you attend each class or group meeting. Most lessons will include the following elements:

Article. Each lesson (except lesson 1) has an article that needs to be read before your class or group meets. The article will get you thinking about key aspects of the upcoming session, or about important elements you need to understand but will not be covered elsewhere. The articles are essential for the course as a whole. Make sure you read each article, answer the accompanying reflection questions, and complete the prayer exercise if there is one, *before your class or group meets*. Sharing what you've learned from the article will be part of each class session. **Allow yourself ample time (usually thirty to forty-five minutes) to read the article and prepare thoughtfully.**

Opening activity. Lessons begin with an activity or discussion that will get your small group or cohort engaged and talking with each other.

Lesson. This is the lecture portion of the class, but it often will include some periods of personal reflection or group work and discussion.

Heart questions. Your group or cohort will take the lesson content you've learned and apply it to your hearts and everyday life. In this way, you will move from simply receiving knowledge to fostering transformation through discussion and sharing in community with others.

Renewal in the gospel. This section allows you to consider how the gospel speaks to your heart and invites you into a deep relationship with God. How is your heart responding to what you've learned? How do you need to believe the good news of Jesus in this situation?

Preparing for the next lesson. You'll be told about the next lesson's article to read. Your class might also be memorizing Scripture or completing other activities between meetings.

Cross-cultural experience. At some point during the course or afterward, you might take part in a cross-cultural experience that will let you live out what you've learned. More information about this is at the start of the leader's section of this book.

In all of this, remember that community is an essential part of the learning process of *You Are Sent*. No matter what the setting (classroom, small group, one-on-one discipleship, etc.), make sharing with others a priority. The content of this course is meant to bring you alongside others who are asking the same questions and exploring God's global mission.

GLOSSARY

This glossary is placed here, before the lessons, to help you understand how this book uses terminology. There can be confusion and disagreement around what terms mean in the world of missions. Use this as a guide to help bring clarity to the course.

church planting. The ministry of evangelism and discipleship that leads to the establishment of new communities of Christians.[1]

diaspora. A reference to people groups living outside their home country, from the Greek word meaning to "scatter about."

evangelical. A broad movement of churches and Christians who hold to salvation by grace through faith in Christ alone, an authoritative and infallible view of the Bible, and are committed to the proclamation of the gospel.

exclusivism. The belief that the only way to God and to eternal life is through the life, death, and resurrection of Jesus, through conscious faith in the work of Christ.

globalization. The growing interconnectedness and interdependence of the world's cultures, countries, and economies.

inclusivism. The belief that although Christianity and the work of Jesus are uniquely true, it is possible to be saved apart from faith in Christ in this lifetime.

mission. Everything the church does that points to God's glory and his kingdom. This term is broader than *missions* and encompasses more than evangelism, discipleship, and church planting, to include all the church is called to do in the world.

missional. A concept that sees evangelism as a way of life—taking on the posture, practices, and habits of a missionary in the everyday rhythms of life.

missions. The work of God's people (the church) to proclaim Jesus, make disciples, and plant new churches. This term is most often used in reference to carrying out these activities cross-culturally.[2]

people group. An ethnic group of people with a distinct language and culture that sets them apart from other groups. In global missions, a people group is the largest group within which the gospel can spread without facing significant barriers of understanding and acceptance due to language, culture, and geography.[3]

pluralism. The belief that all paths in life lead to God, and that Jesus and the truths of Christianity are not unique.

renewal mission. A perspective of living on mission that values being rooted in the love of God, moving out toward others with the gospel, and then coming back to find renewal in Christ over and over again. This cycle of renewal and mission connects what God is doing *in* us with what he is doing *through* us.

unreached people group. A people group with little access to the gospel and where churches and Christians are too few to effectively reach their own people without outside assistance. This is often defined as less than 2 percent of the population being followers of Jesus.

urban. A geographic place where people choose to live and work in close proximity to other people,[4] creating many daily person-to-person interactions.[5] The words *urban* and *city* are often used as synonyms.

urbanization. The reality that our world is progressively urban, with more than half of its population now living in cities.

wrath. An attribute of God that reveals his intense hatred toward sin and his readiness to fully punish those who do not repent of their sin and rebellion.[6]

1

GOD'S GLOBAL MISSION IN THE OLD TESTAMENT

*The Bible is from start to finish a missionary book, for it is the
story of God himself reaching into human history to reconcile a
fallen and rebellious humanity to himself and to reestablish his
reign over all creation.*
— Encountering Theology of Mission[1]

BIG IDEA

From before the beginning of time, God has had a plan for reaching all
nations and peoples of the earth with the gospel. The first two sessions
will walk through Scripture passages from Genesis through Revelation
to unveil God's love and pursuit of all nations, to lay a deeply rooted
theological foundation that missions is a whole-Bible idea, and to show
that reaching every nation, tribe, and tongue is at the very heart of God.

OPENING ACTIVITY

At the top of a paper, write your name, your hometown, and your favorite place in the world. Then answer the following questions, or others
provided by your leader, individually on your paper.

What's one thing about yourself that sounds like a lie but is totally true?

What book or movie has helped shape your life?

What is an event in your life that's impacted you deeply?

What's one thing you hope to gain from this class?

Finally, draw a picture that symbolizes what God is doing in your life right now.

Now gather as a cohort, or in pairs, and have each person share their responses.

LESSON

This session's lesson will take you through the Old Testament, showing how global missions is not a new idea but has been God's plan all along. (If you are teaching this lesson, consult the leader's material in the second half of this book.)

HEART QUESTIONS

* Discuss these questions within your group or cohort. They are intended to apply the teaching you just heard to your heart. Seek to be open and honest with each other and develop genuine community. Try to foster trust and good conversation.

As you walked through the Old Testament in this lesson, what truths about God and his missional heart grabbed you, and why?

As we begin this study of God's global mission, what burdens do you carry? How can the group be praying for you?

RENEWAL IN THE GOSPEL

✳ Read this reflection as a group, in your cohort, or to yourself. Then take a few minutes to write some brief answers to the questions. If parts of your answers would be helpful to others, share and discuss them when you're done. This section's purpose is to help you stay grounded in Christ and the gospel so that, as you move forward in mission, your confidence and comfort are in Jesus and this renews you daily.

As we've been seeing, the Bible is a seamless, whole grand narrative—the One True Story that takes in all of history. That story is all about the unchanging loving purpose of our unchanging God, working itself out in space and time. As we immerse ourselves in that story, we come to understand better and better who we are and what we were made for.

But often we functionally live in an alternative, rival story of our own imagining—a story that revolves around our personal goals and fears. That story can seem more "real" than God's story.

Living missional lives requires us to be anchored in God's story. In order to do that, it's helpful for us to learn to articulate something of the rival

Lesson 1: God's Global Mission in the Old Testament 9

story that can be so powerful for each of us. Telling that story—about the worldly fears and achievements that seem more real than God's work—can be part of what God uses to "declaw" it and rob it of its power.

Take a few minutes now to journal about these things or write some brief notes. You can use one or more of these questions to guide you:

- In your alternate story, whom do you want to be?

- What current struggles in your life define the storyline? (What do you fear that you're struggling to avoid, or what goals are you struggling to achieve?)

- What do you imagine your "happy ending" to look like?

- And how is this story connected to God's story? Is your story in step with God's story, or in competition with it?

When your group is ready, share some of what you wrote if you are comfortable doing so.

GROUP PRAYER

Pray for one another as you end this class. Ask God to work deeply in you and within those in your cohort to show you his deep love for the nations and your place in expanding the kingdom of God.

PREPARING FOR THE NEXT LESSON

Read and reflect. On your own, before the next time your group meets, read the article "Renewing Mission," which comes next in this book. Also answer the questions at the end of that article, and be prepared to share your answers at the next meeting. **Allow at least 30 minutes for this preparation.**

Memorize. If your class is memorizing Scripture, learn Malachi 1:11.

> "For from the rising of the sun to its setting my name will be great among the nations, and in every place incense will be offered to my name, and a pure offering. For my name will be great among the nations, says the LORD of hosts."

Activity. If your leader assigns this activity or if it sounds helpful to you, take some time this week to watch a documentary or film from another culture and language. What did you learn? How are you inspired to pray for that culture?

FURTHER RESOURCES

» *Salvation to the Ends of the Earth* by Andreas J. Köstenberger

» *Mission in the Old Testament* by Walter C. Kaiser Jr.

» *The Mission of God* by Christopher J. H. Wright

Lesson

ARTICLE

1

RENEWING MISSION

To prepare for LESSON 2, read this article ahead of time and answer the questions that follow. *Note: This article was written by Serge staff and missionaries, compiled by Margaret-Elliotte Rebello, and adapted by the author. It is used with permission.*

When we speak of *renewal mission*, we mean this: God desires to see his kingdom come both in our own hearts (renewal) and in the world (missions), and these happen together.

We know that the gospel is meant to work in our own hearts, driving us closer to God through repentance and faith (Mark 1:15; Acts 19:4). We also know that the gospel drives us out in love for others through evangelism, discipleship, good works, and our even our presence. However, we often consider our personal growth in repentance and faith and going out on mission as two separate things. We live as though God works in our hearts, and then at a separate time and place we go and "do missions."

But the gospel is much more dynamic than that. True worship is a heart-soul-and-mind experience that draws us *into* greater intimacy with God and at the same time *out* in love toward others (Matthew 22:37–40). True and lasting mission for God and to others must flow from a life rooted in relationship with God and renewed in him daily. And likewise, deep and daily renewal usually happens when we see our need for God because we are engaged in real mission.

Renewal and missions drive each other. As the gospel takes hold in our own hearts, we are naturally drawn into God's work in the world. And God's work in the world naturally calls us back to our own deep need for him and his deep love for us. Renewal keeps leading to more mission, and mission keeps leading to more renewal.

Let's start with how doing missions leads to renewal in our lives. You may be familiar with the saying that "doing mission work is like pouring Miracle-Gro® on your sins." It doesn't mean mission work makes us inherently more sinful (though new sin struggles may arise). But still, there's something about stepping out in faith to share the gospel and make disciples that means our hearts will be tempted, our understanding of our weakness will increase, and the depth of our need for the Savior will be magnified.

Loving people is hard, and our sinful nature makes it even more difficult. As we see how unloving we are and how difficult it is to love others, we become even more aware of our need for God to work in our lives. We learn that the world is deeply broken and that we are so much more sinful than we thought.

This causes us to turn afresh to the good news of Jesus: God does not leave us in our sin. He justifies us, adopts us as his children, calls us his own, and gives us the Holy Spirit as an agent of continual growth in our lives (1 John 3:2; Romans 8:16). We are renewed in the confidence that as we go out on mission to others, to share Jesus and make disciples, God promises to go with us (Matthew 28:20). We are his beloved children (1 John 3:1). Our need for God is so much deeper than we imagine, but we are also so much more loved than we could ever know!

Now notice how this gospel renewal leads us back into missions. It is in this place of deeper reliance on God, as broken sinners in continual need of grace, that God sends us out into the world (Ephesians 2:10). It is not our expert knowledge, energetic personality, or passionate evangelism that qualify us as missionaries. *It is our need for God that qualifies us.* And it is nothing other than God's abounding love and grace that allows us to come alongside others and point them to Jesus.

As we experience our deep need for God and his even deeper love for us, we are able to lead others to the feet of Jesus, the one who provides everlasting life. This dual perspective, seeing the depth of our sin and the height of God's love for us, is what grounds us and drives us out on mission to others.

For example, here's how this renewal-mission dynamic might play out in the lives of a Christian couple who decide to adopt a child or become foster parents: Their commitment to welcome children in need is rooted in God's love, the love they have experienced personally. That love drives them out toward others in compassion and service, and they welcome a child into their family. However, parenting children is hard, and parenting children from traumatic backgrounds is especially difficult. By stepping into adoption and foster care, they uncover "new" personal sins—impatience, insecurity, issues of control—they hadn't dealt with before. As they struggle to parent and wrestle with their newly-revealed sin, they see their need for Jesus more deeply. They draw near to God and experience anew his provision and his great love for them and their children. This renewal experience brings refreshment and courage to keep going.

This is how God's kingdom comes both in the world (a needy child is loved) and in our hearts (parents learn patience and reliance on God) at the same time. This renewal-mission dynamic is not just for adoptive and foster parents or for cross-cultural missionaries living on the margins of the world. God's renewing love is available to everyone.

HOW RENEWAL IS CONNECTED TO MISSION IN THE BIBLE

The rhythm of renewal and missions is seen throughout the life of Jesus as he moves out in love toward others and also retreats to spend time abiding with his Father. For example, after Jesus fed the five thousand, "Immediately he made the disciples get into the boat and go before him to the other side, while he dismissed the crowds. And after he had dismissed the crowds, he went up on the mountain by himself to pray. When evening came, he was there alone" (Matthew 14:22–23). In fact, Jesus's times of intense ministry are often paralleled by his times of intense connection with God (see Matthew 4:1–11; 17:1–9; 26:36–46; Mark 1:35; Luke 6:12).

God longs to be in relationship with us as we are in relationship with others. Paul notes the connection between renewal and missions as he states, "It is God who works in you, both to will and to work for his good pleasure" (Philippians 2:13). Not only is God working to renew our hearts and drive us out to do kingdom work, it is "for his good pleasure." How incredible is that? God is pleased to do this work in our lives and in the world. And in his infinite power and endless mercy, he provides for us all that we need for life in every moment.

Both missions and renewal are personal, local, corporate, and global. Jesus told his disciples, "Go into all the world and proclaim the gospel to the whole creation" (Mark 16:15). God's work includes all the world, the whole creation, including you and me. Paul wrote, "The whole creation has been groaning together in the pains of childbirth until now. And not only the creation, but we ourselves, who have the firstfruits of the Spirit, groan inwardly as we wait eagerly for adoption as sons, the redemption of our bodies" (Romans 8:22–23).

Jesus says, "Behold, I am making all things new" (Revelation 21:5). *All things* truly means all things: your heart, your mind, your body, your relationships, your neighborhood, your community, your nation, and the entire world!

Your personal renewal is about both what God is doing *in* you and also what he is doing *through* you. This is what it means to be on mission with God for the good of others. Your personal Christian growth is not just about you; it is also how God is using you in the people around you and in the community where you live. God's plan is to use you, his child, in the work of redeeming the world. "For the creation was subjected to futility, not willingly, but because of him who subjected it, in hope that the creation itself will be set free from its bondage to corruption and obtain the freedom of the glory of the children of God" (Romans 8:20–21).

We cannot and should not reduce the gospel to being just about personal sanctification, nor should we make it merely a social gospel that comes in service for others with no change in our own lives. God calls us and the church globally to be a sign, instrument, and foretaste of the kingdom of God. As a sign, we point others toward a love relationship with God. As an instrument, we bring hope, justice, and peace into the world. And as a foretaste, we demonstrate to others a small part of what God's ultimate plan is for the world: a new heaven and new earth.[2]

REFLECT

Take time now to reflect, pray, and write down some responses to the following questions. Be ready to share some of your thoughts when your group meets.

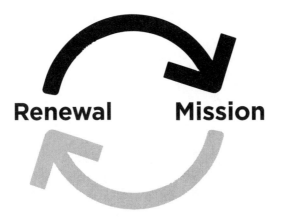

Look again at the diagram above, and think about how it is at work in your life. How does your growth in the gospel (renewal) propel you out to others (mission)? And how does your service of God and others (mission) drive you back to rest in the gospel (renewal)?

How might this renewal-mission dynamic shape the way you think about living on mission?

2

GOD'S GLOBAL MISSION IN THE NEW TESTAMENT

There are lots of stories in the Bible, but all the stories are telling one Big Story. The Story of how God loves his children and comes to rescue them. It takes the whole Bible to tell this Story. And at the center of the Story, there is a baby. Every Story in the Bible whispers his name.
—**Sally Lloyd-Jones**[1]

BIG IDEA

Having seen how God's passionate love for all nations unfolds in the Old Testament, in this lesson we will continue our journey of understanding God's global mission. We will see how it reaches fullness in the New Testament and how God's church is given the charge to go and make disciples of all nations.

OPENING ACTIVITIES

Gather as a group or in your cohort and share your thoughts about the article, "Renewing Mission." How has your delight in the gospel propelled you out on mission, and how has your mission made you hungry for more of the gospel?

LESSON

This session's lesson will take you through the New Testament, showing how God's global mission comes to fulfillment in that part of the Bible. At a point in the lesson, you will discuss the following questions about John 4 within your group:

- As you read this story, what stands out to you about how Jesus engaged with the Samaritan woman and led her to understand the gospel?
- How did the gospel impact this woman and her community and why is this story so important for understanding God's love for the nations?

HEART QUESTIONS

As you've seen the gospel moving in people and places throughout this lesson, what story or passage most moved you, and why?

As you've learned of God's love for all nations, how are you experiencing the love of God in your own life right now? Or if you're struggling to feel God's love, share about that.

RENEWAL IN THE GOSPEL

As we've studied the various Scripture passages in our first two lessons, we've reflected on *what God has done* in the past through Christ to bring about salvation for sinners as well as *what he will do* in the future to bring it to consummation. We've also gotten a glimpse of *what he is doing* in the present to propel his saving purposes forward in the world.

The Bible talks about your salvation too in all three ways. It is something finished: God has saved you (Ephesians 2:8). It is something to anticipate: he will save you (Philippians 1:28). And it is something that is happening now: he is saving you (1 Corinthians 1:18). Your justification is secure, but the implications of the gospel are still being worked out in your life. The Holy Spirit is applying the gospel to you now in time and space, pressing grace into the broken places of your life. And that happens in part as you are involved with him in mission, inviting others to share with you in God's grace.

Take a few minutes to journal or make some notes about this. Consider these questions:

- What has the Holy Spirit already done in your life, and what is he doing now?

- How does engagement with God's mission fit into his ongoing rescue of you?

When your group is ready, share some of what you wrote if you are comfortable doing so.

GROUP PRAYER

Pray that God would use each of you to do ministry among the nations that results in him doing "far more abundantly than all that we ask or think, according to the power at work within us" (Ephesians 3:20).

PREPARING FOR THE NEXT LESSON

Read and reflect. On your own, before the next time your group meets, read the article "God's Wrath Against Sin," which comes next in this book. Also answer the questions within that article, and be prepared to discuss them with the group at the next meeting. **Give yourself at least 45 minutes to do this preparation.**

Memorize. If your class is memorizing Scripture, learn Matthew 28:18–20.

> And Jesus came and said to them, "All authority in heaven and on earth has been given to me. Go therefore and make disciples of all nations, baptizing them in the name of the Father and of the Son and of the Holy Spirit, teaching them to observe all that I have commanded you. And behold, I am with you always, to the end of the age."

Activity. If your leader assigns it, or if it sounds helpful to you, take some time this week to explore a new neighborhood. If possible, make it a neighborhood with people who come from other countries or one out of your comfort zone. Pray for the neighborhood as you walk the streets. Ask God to work in you and in those you see around you. Look for opportunities to meet and talk to the people who live there. Look for opportunities to share Jesus with others. Consider doing this activity as a cohort or with another person.

FURTHER RESOURCES

» *Let the Nations Be Glad* by John Piper

» *Introducing World Missions* by Scott Moreau, Gary Corwin, and Gary McGee

» *A Biblical Theology of Missions* by George Peters

ARTICLE

GOD'S WRATH AGAINST SIN

To prepare for LESSON 3, read this article ahead of time and answer the Bible study questions within it.

"Do you think I will go to hell?" These words still ring in my ears. I was a sophomore in high school, seeking to love Jesus, and doing my dead-level best to make him known to those around me. One of my good friends sat beside me in computer class. She was a girl from India, a nominal Hindu from a Hindu family, and she was beginning to understand what I believed about the gospel. We would often talk between assignments about all kinds of things. It was during one of these conversations that she asked me the question, "Do you think I will go to hell when I die?" I honestly didn't know what to say. By this point in our friendship, she knew exactly what I believed about this question. Why else would I share the gospel with her and urge her to run to Jesus unless I believed that her fate was an eternity without God? After a long, awkward pause I answered yes, and I urged her to place her faith in Jesus.

What comes to mind when you think about God's wrath and the concept of hell? Maybe you think of a hateful street preacher you've encountered. Perhaps you grimace at the thought of God's judgment in light of his love. Wherever connotation you have, I think we can all agree that coming to grips with the wrath of God and the reality of hell is difficult.

When we are talking about God's wrath in this lesson, we are referring to his attitude toward sin and evil and the necessity of punishing sinful people unless we take refuge in him by faith in Christ.[2] As hard as it may be, it is essential that we wrestle with these truths and allow them to undergird what we believe about local and global missions. For missions to be a necessary endeavor, we must firmly believe that God does indeed have wrath against our sin and that those who live in unrepentant rebellion will face an eternity apart from him. When we see God's wrath against sin clearly, we see how desperately both we and others need the good news of Christ Jesus. When we understand his wrath against sin, it makes his love and work on the cross that much more amazing.

It is important to know that God's wrath (his anger against sin) is not the same kind of anger we exhibit as broken, sinful people. Our anger is often an uncontrolled and destructive emotion because it comes from our sinful hearts—out of jealousy, irritability, pride, or self-centeredness. But God's wrath only comes from his perfect character. All that God is and does (including his wrath) is good, holy, and right. Instead of thinking of God's wrath against sin as a negative, we need to set our minds on the truth that God's wrath and judgment are right and good because they are an outworking of his justice and love.

Imagine you're in a courtroom watching a trial play out. A criminal who has been found guilty of a long list of crimes stands before the judge. He has not just committed one crime but a lifetime of clear and horrific rebellion against the law. He is guilty, without a doubt, and deserving of punishment. Would it be wrong for the judge to punish him for the crimes he committed? No, the judge's duty is to set wrong things right by bringing justice to unjust situations. In a similar way, God's wrath and judgment against sin reflect his commitment to bring about justice for those who suffer: "O LORD, you hear the desire of the afflicted; you will strengthen their heart; you will incline your ear to do justice to the fatherless and the oppressed, so that man who is of the earth may strike terror no more" (Psalm 10:17–18).

✳ Stop for a moment to read and reflect. Read Nahum 1:2–8, which tells about God's judgment of the wicked. Write down your answers

Lesson 2: God's Global Mission in the New Testament 23

to the following questions, and be prepared to discuss them the next time your group meets.

- What is God's response to those who rebel against him? Write down some details from the passage.

- What is your natural response to reading this passage and studying God's wrath? What is difficult for you to come to grips with?

- What are some reasons why verse 7 is an important, clarifying part of the passage?

- What aspects of God's character are highlighted in this passage? How do they help you understand God's anger against our sin?

The stories of God's wrath against sin and evil can be overwhelming, but they are foundational to understanding the gospel. Jesus intentionally took on a human nature and became flesh so that he could bear the entire weight of God's wrath for us on the cross. He literally became sin for us. In doing so, he appeased God's wrath so that we do not have to suffer it, and in doing so made a way for us to be reconciled with God. There is no gospel, no path to real and eternal life, without Christ first suffering judgment in our place.

God's wrath shows us that he takes our sin seriously. And because our sin is serious, we need Christ so that we can be in relationship with our holy God. Look how he has loved us and the nations: "But God shows his love for us in that while we were still sinners, Christ died for us. Since, therefore, we have now been justified by his blood, much more shall we be saved by him from the wrath of God. For if while we were enemies we were reconciled to God by the death of his Son, much more, now that we are reconciled, shall we be saved by his life" (Romans 5:8–10).

At its core, missions is taking the love and truth of Jesus's death and resurrection to people who do not have it. Missions is calling people away from their sin (and from living under God's wrath) and into eternity with him. The beauty and necessity of missions is that God in his love provides a way back to life with him. Stephen Strauss puts it well:

> In his love God has provided a way for all humankind to enjoy fellowship with him. But the Bible's teaching is clear: some people will persist in their rejection of God and as a result will condemn themselves to an eternity of separation from him. . . . Hell is a real place and its misery will be the eternal state of all those who reject God's revelation of himself and choose to follow the rebellious inclinations of their own will.[3]

As hard as these truths are to hear, it's vital for us to run to Scripture and embrace the realities that God's wrath will be poured out against sin and that God's grace, through faith in Jesus, allows us to be saved from his wrath into a relationship with God. Those who do not follow Jesus will spend an eternity in hell away from God's presence. God's response to this dreadful reality was to send his son Jesus as a redeeming sacrifice for people from all nations of the earth, including you and me. Inviting others to follow Jesus is inviting them *from* the wrath of God and *to* the incredible riches that come when we live with God through his grace. Although you're far worse than you think, God's love for you is far greater than you could ever imagine!

When you share the gospel, you are inviting others to take shelter in the love and sacrifice of Jesus. In Christ, you are saved from the wrath of God and are adopted as his son or daughter, given a full inheritance in Christ. As you look at the depth of your sin and the height of God's love, you must share the gospel with both urgency and joy because missions is necessary. But more than simply being necessary, it is a joyful experience when you share the gospel with others. Think about it. Not only are you the recipient of God's love, being saved from wrath, but you are the messenger of that same love to others. In his kindness, the objects of his wrath become the conduits of his love. Simply amazing.

Lesson

3

NECESSITY OF MISSIONS

"Enter by the narrow gate. For the gate is wide and the way is easy that leads to destruction, and those who enter by it are many. For the gate is narrow and the way is hard that leads to life, and those who find it are few."
—Matthew 7:13–14

BIG IDEA

The work of missions is necessary because, apart from Jesus, there is no hope of eternal life. Those who do not follow Christ will spend eternity in hell separated from God. But through his grace, God provides a way from death to life through his Son so that we can be in a restored relationship with him.

OPENING ACTIVITIES

In groups, discuss the article, "God's Wrath Against Sin." What was your response to reading about God's wrath in Nahum 1:2–8? What aspects of God's character in that passage made an impact on you, and why?

Also read Matthew 25:31–46 in your group. Discuss: What does Jesus have to say about God's judgment? About hell?

Finally, take some time as a group to pray before the lesson begins. These are hard issues for anyone to wrestle with and we need to ask the Spirit to meet us in this moment. Ask the Lord to:

- Make his truth clear to you from his Word and through the power of the Holy Spirit.
- Be willing to be open and listen to what God is showing you through the Scriptures.

LESSON

This session's lesson will examine how faith in Jesus is the only way to eternal life, and how this brings urgency to the work of missions.

HEART QUESTIONS

After working through this lesson, how do you better understand or appreciate the just nature of God's wrath?

Who are the people in your life who do not have a saving faith in Jesus? How might this lesson change or challenge how you relate to them?

RENEWAL IN THE GOSPEL

First John 2:1–2 says, "We have an advocate with the Father, Jesus Christ the righteous. He is the propitiation for our sins." *Propitiation* is sometimes translated as "atoning sacrifice," a sacrifice that satisfies the wrath of God.

As you reflect on the weighty content of this week's lesson, give a place in your thoughts to consider what it means for you to have an advocate with the Father who is the propitiation for your sins. Imagine what it would be like to have no such advocate, and to have to answer to God yourself for everything you have done and said and thought in your heart. Journal for a few minutes, or write some notes, in response to these questions:

- What does it mean to you to have an advocate who is the propitiation for your sins, and what emotions does it stir in you?

- How does thinking about these things affect the way you think about others?

When your group is ready, share some of what you wrote if you are comfortable doing so.

GROUP PRAYER

Take time to talk to God about any ways you have been challenged by this lesson. Perhaps you need to repent of the ways you fall into pluralist or inclusivist thinking rather than respecting the exclusivity of Christ. Or perhaps you need to talk to God about how you struggle to understand his wrath.

Pray for those in your life and community who do not know Jesus, and praise God for the incredible mercy he has shown us through Christ.

PREPARING FOR THE NEXT LESSON

Read and reflect. On your own, before the next time your group meets, read the article "God on the Move," which comes next in this book. Also answer the questions at the end of that article, and be prepared to share your answers at the next meeting. **Allow at least 30 minutes for this preparation.**

Memorize. If your class is memorizing Scripture, learn Acts 4:12.

> And there is salvation in no one else, for there is no other name under heaven given among men by which we must be saved.

Activity. If your leader assigns it or if it sounds helpful to you, visit an international restaurant this week. Preferably, pick one of a culture you are not very familiar with. Order a dish off the menu that is unique to that culture and ask your server about the dish. Learn your server's name and do your best to learn as much as you can about their culture. Consider doing this activity as a cohort or with another person.

FURTHER RESOURCES

» *Jesus: The Only Way to God* by John Piper

» *Encountering Theology of Mission* by Craig Ott, Stephen J. Strauss, and Timothy C. Tennent

» *Knowing God* by J. I. Packer, "God and Judge" and "The Wrath of God"

Lesson

ARTICLE

GOD ON THE MOVE

To prepare for LESSON 4, read this article ahead of time and answer the questions that follow.

Missions history is so complex, so beautiful, and yet so disturbing at the same time. The history of the church is filled with beautiful stories that magnify God's name alongside stories of sin and abuse within the church. We could spend a lifetime studying missions history and still not fully understand it in all its complexity. But at the end of the day, the history of missions is nothing more and nothing less than the history of God's faithfulness to use broken people to reach those who don't yet know him.

This article will focus on the period known as *early missions*, which refers to global missions expansion from the time of the New Testament church to the middle of the 1700s. The teaching time in your upcoming class will focus on *modern missions*, which refers to the time of Protestant missions from the middle of the 1700s until today. Together, these periods can be subdivided into five epochs defined by church historian Ralph Winter.[1]

One of the most fascinating things we'll notice in church history is how the epicenter of Christianity has moved around the world. In the Gospels and the book of Acts, the home base of Christianity clearly is Jerusalem. This is where Jesus was murdered, where he rose from the grave to defeat death, and where the Holy Spirit came to launch the worldwide missionary expansion. But Jerusalem did not stay the epicenter of Christianity. In God's providence, he has moved it around the world. Pastor and missiologist Brad Bell has said, "True Christendom is only realized in heaven. Missions history reminds us that when we've lost the willingness to risk in the cause of Christ, the kingdom has most likely moved past us."[2]

So, the history of missions is a history of God on the move. It is a story of God showing his power and glory to a watching world and fulfilling the mission he gave the church.

AGE OF THE ROMANS (NEW TESTAMENT–400S)

The first epoch or age is the age of the Romans. This starts with the life, death, and resurrection of the greatest missionary to ever live, Jesus himself. He embodied the model of the perfect missionary. Before his ascension into heaven, Jesus gathered his disciples on a mountain in Galilee and gave them a marching order that would guide the church for all of history: "Go therefore and make disciples of all nations, baptizing them in the name of the Father and of the Son and of the Holy Spirit, teaching them to observe all that I have commanded you. And behold, I am with you always, to the end of the age" (Matthew 28:19–20).

From that small group of followers at Jesus's resurrection, God began a movement that would spread around the world. We know from Acts 2 that right after Pentecost there were three thousand followers of Jesus. By the end of the first century, there were around ten thousand believers. By AD 300, there were an estimated six million. Humanly speaking the impossible had happened: Christians could be found in every major city and province in the known world because of the way God was at work through his people.[3]

Even when opposition was fierce, God continued to grow his kingdom. As a result of the early disciples being scattered because of persecution, God raised up a multicultural, multiethnic church in Antioch, in modern-day Syria. From this unlikely church, global missions really began. Acts 13:1–4 tells the story of the church in Antioch sending out two of their elders, Barnabas and Saul, as missionaries to reach the Mediterranean world. "After fasting and praying they laid their hands on them and sent them off. So, being sent out by the Holy Spirit, they went down to Seleucia, and from there they sailed to Cyprus" (v. 4).

From Antioch, this movement of missions not only reached westward but soon also moved eastward toward Edessa, an ancient city that lies in modern-day Turkey. There are many beautiful and often untold stories of how God sent missionaries and grew his church in the Eastern world. In fact, historian Ed Smither writes, "In the first eight centuries of the church, the gospel traveled much further east than it did west."[4]

Alongside Antioch, God used many of the early Christians to take the gospel to unreached places. We see Christians like Paul, Timothy, Silas, Aquila and Priscilla, and others begin taking the gospel all over the Roman Empire. Christian tradition also tells how many of the apostles did gospel ministry in places around the world, including Thomas who did missionary work in India.[5]

In less than three hundred years, the gospel went from a cave in Jerusalem to a palace in Rome. The Spirit used practical conditions to help men and women take the gospel to new places.[6] The Roman Empire had built a massive system of roads. Greek was the common language throughout the region. And Jews were living in many parts of the empire, where they had established synagogues and attracted God-fearing Gentiles who readily welcomed the gospel when it arrived.

In this way, the gospel also moved through North Africa and the Middle East. Although these are some of the least-reached places on earth today, at one time they were filled with faithful followers of Jesus. Some of history's greatest theologians came from North Africa and the Middle East: Athanasius from Egypt, Ignatius from Syria, Tertullian from Tunisia, and Augustine from Algeria.

AGE OF THE BARBARIANS (400s–800s)

The second age of missions history is the age of the barbarians. During this time, the epicenter of Christianity moved from Rome to Constantinople, modern-day Istanbul. Barbarians began conquering the Romans in the fifth century. If the Romans were slow to take the gospel to the barbarians, then God would bring the barbarians to them.

Missionary Profile: Patrick

Shrouded in mystery, St. Patrick is one of the most misrepresented characters in church history. He was not a Catholic nor an Irishman, but he was a man used by God to impact many with the gospel.[7]

At age sixteen, Patrick was captured from his home in the Roman province of Britain and made a slave in Ireland. He was held for six years under brutal labor. After finally escaping and returning to his homeland, he was drawn back to Ireland by the gripping memory of his former slave masters' need for Jesus. The people were so bewildered by his return that they welcomed him. He eventually established a remarkable church presence. He developed and used missionary methods that are still used in mission practice today.

Patrick saw significant success in his ministry. He helped plant two hundred churches and saw an estimated 100,000 people turn to Christ and be baptized.[8] His ministry was not without suffering, however. On numerous occasions he faced persecution from those who opposed the gospel.[9] Patrick's legacy as an early missionary who deeply impacted Ireland is also is a reminder of the power of the gospel to set *both* the oppressed *and* their oppressors free.

The gospel also continued to spread through early monastic leaders like Columba and Boniface. These men helped create monasteries that were more like missionary training centers than holy hideouts.[10] From these early monasteries, monks took the gospel out to the surrounding communities and throughout the region.

AGE OF THE VIKINGS (800s–1200s)

The third age was the age of the Vikings. During this time, the center of Christianity moved from Constantinople to Scandinavia. Vikings were ruthless people who brutalized men, women, children, and churches. Yet even as the church was being brutalized, some Vikings were compelled by the gospel and believed. Winter writes, "In God's eyes, [the Vikings'] redemption must have been more important than the harrowing tragedy of this new invasion of barbarian violence and evil which fell upon God's own people whom He loved."[11] The conversion of the Vikings is a stark reminder that throughout history God redeems and uses the most unlikely of people to grow his kingdom.

AGE OF THE CRUSADES (1200s–1600s)

The fourth age is the infamous age of the Crusades. Here the hub of Christianity shifted from Scandinavia to all of Europe. The warring culture of the Vikings combined with Catholicism to create a strange militant religiosity and a desire to retake the Holy Land from Muslim control. Sadly, most all of Europe rallied to this cause and the church shifted its focus from worship to war and territorial conquest.

But there were exceptions to the warring movement in the European church. One of the bright spots in this dark time for missions was Raymond Lull and his passion to see Muslims know Jesus. Lull represents a contingent of faithful Christians who continued to demonstrate and declare the gospel to others.

Missionary Profile: Raymond Lull

Called "the apostle of love," Raymond Lull braved North Africa (modern-day Tunisia and Algeria) with the gospel rather than the sword. Lull studied the Arab language and culture for nine years before taking several extended trips into North Africa to evangelize and disciple new Christians. Each time he was rejected and banished. During his last journey, he was stoned to death by an angry mob. Though his ministry in North Africa didn't bear much visible fruit, Lull's efforts remind us that in every generation God has raised up faithful people who are willing to leave the comfort of their own culture, and step into the sacrifice and danger, so that the message of the gospel moves forward.

Faithful efforts of men like Lull were vastly overshadowed by the misguided, bloodthirsty Crusades. These were dark days for the Western church, but God was still at work through men and women like Lull and others.

AGE OF THE ENDS OF THE EARTH (1700s–PRESENT DAY)

The final age Ralph Winter identifies is the age of the "ends of the earth." Within this timeframe, the epicenter of Christianity decentralized from Europe and resettled in North America. This happened through two primary means: the Protestant Reformation and overseas conquest. The teaching time in the upcoming lesson will tell more about this age.

REFLECT

As you read and study missions history, it is important to remember that history is more than just the retelling of facts. It is the flesh-and-blood story of how a loving God uses flawed and broken sinners to bring his message of salvation to those who don't yet know Jesus. Reflecting on these stories should give us the courage to continue stepping out in faith, trusting that God is at work even now to gather his people from every tongue, tribe, and nation.

Take time to reflect, pray, and write down some responses to the following questions. Be ready to share some of your thoughts when your group meets.

How does God's work in the past inspire you to live today? What stories from missions history, or church history in general, move you toward a deeper life with God and toward life on mission for others?

4

HISTORY OF MISSIONS

The Church of the first Christian generation was a genuinely
missionary Church. . . . What is clear is that every Christian was
a witness. Where there were Christians, there would be a living
faith, and before long an expanding Christian Community.
—Stephen Neill[1]

BIG IDEA

Missions history is simply the history of the church. The gospel has
moved from Jerusalem outward to the ends of the earth over a period
of two thousand years. The story of missions is full of people, churches,
and movements that, through God's grace and power, turned the world
upside down.

OPENING ACTIVITIES

Gather as a cohort, or in pairs, and have each person share their responses
to the reflection questions from the article, "God on the Move."

How does God's work in the past inspire you to live today? What stories
from missions history, or church history in general, move you toward a
deeper life with God and toward life on mission?

Someone might visit to talk about how they share their faith in everyday
life.

LESSON

This session's lesson will be a continuation of your study of the history of missions, focusing on the modern missions movement.

HEART QUESTIONS

As you consider the stories of missionaries told in this lesson, what might God be teaching you about how he works through both success and failure in life?

What is God doing in your own heart as you reflect on God's movement throughout history?

RENEWAL IN THE GOSPEL

What has been stirred in your heart as you've read and heard about missionaries of the past? For some of us, stories like these are thrilling and attractive; they stir us up to want to be like the men and women who went before us. But if we're honest, we'll admit that attraction often comes with mixed motives. Although we may have a genuine heart for people to know Christ, and for God to get glory, at the same time there's an undercurrent of longing to *be someone* and to live the kind of life that will cause others to admire us—maybe to tell our story after we're gone. In short, our hearts want some glory too, and we wonder whether missions might be a way to get it.

Or maybe you hear these stories and think, *What in the world could this have to do with me? I'm no one special. I could never do anything like that.* You're painfully aware of your weakness and inadequacy, of past failures and disappointments. And hearing about heroic missionaries of the past doesn't help.

These are things to talk to the Lord about. Take some time now to write about where your thoughts have gone. Perhaps write a prayer in which you tell Jesus about these things. Give him access to your heart, to your inner monologues. Confess your sins and tell him your fears.

When your group is done writing, share some of what you wrote if you are comfortable doing so.

GROUP PRAYER

Pray together for the future of missions and your individual roles in it. Ask that God would continue to shape your hearts for missions.

PREPARING FOR THE NEXT LESSON

Read and reflect. On your own, before the next time your group meets, read the article "Abide with God," which comes next in this book. Also answer the questions and complete the prayer exercise at the end of that article, and be prepared to share at the next meeting. **Allow 45 minutes to an hour for this preparation so that your prayer is unhurried.**

Memorize. If your class is memorizing Scripture, learn Acts 2:42–47.

> And they devoted themselves to the apostles' teaching and the fellowship, to the breaking of bread and the prayers. And awe came upon every soul, and many wonders and signs were being done through the apostles. And all who believed were together and had all things in common. And they were selling their possessions and belongings and distributing the proceeds to all, as any had need. And day by day, attending the temple together and breaking bread in their homes, they received their food with glad and generous hearts, praising God and having favor with all the people. And the Lord added to their number day by day those who were being saved.

Activity. If your leader assigns it or if it sounds helpful to you, read a missionary biography. As you read, ask yourself how you can invest your life in missions in a way that will help push back the darkness?

FURTHER RESOURCES

» *Christian Mission: A Concise Global History* by Edward Smither

» *From Jerusalem to Irian Jaya: A Biographical History of Christian Missions* by Ruth Tucker

» *A History of Christian Missions* by Stephen Neill

Lesson

ARTICLE

ABIDE WITH GOD

To prepare for LESSON 5, read this article ahead of time and answer the questions and complete the prayer exercise that follows.

Talk to any cross-cultural missionary who has been on the field for a while, and they will tell you that the most important aspect of living on mission is abiding with God—rooting your life in God through regular communion with him. A life well-lived for mission is a life rooted in and overflowing from a life with God. Simply put, our mission work should flow out of our real and intimate communion with God.

But what does abiding with God look like? The abiding life is a life that prioritizes *being* over *doing*. It is a life that finds its primary identity and fulfillment in relationship with Christ. Simply put, a person whose life is marked by abiding with God prioritizes being with, depending on, and enjoying God above all else. Let me suggest two ways to think practically about it.

1. Embrace a life of communion. We often think that abiding with God can be simplified to practicing a handful of spiritual disciples. Although spiritual disciples are essential to our relationship with God (as we will see later), there is more to the Christian life—namely, walking with and depending on the Holy Spirit daily.

Think of communing with God as walking with a friend through your neighborhood. You talk about things that matter to you and enjoy one another's company. You walk together unconcerned about time or destination, but instead enjoy your friend's presence. Communion with God is like this but even more so. God walks with us in the highs and lows of life. He is present when we wake up to screaming kids in the morning and when we go to sleep fearful that we are not enough. God walks with us when loneliness sets in and when we fail over and over again. He is also present in the mundane moments of life—driving to work, walking the dog, paying a bill. To walk with God, to embrace the abiding life, is to become more fully aware of his constant presence and to embrace this wonderful reality.

2. Practice the disciplines. As we walk daily with God, enjoying him and depending on him in the everyday moments of life, we are also called to practice spiritual habits or disciplines. These allow us to grow a deeper relationship with God. They are not to-do-list items to check off, but invitations to enjoy Jesus. For Christians, these disciplines become pathways to a fuller life.

John Starke articulates this need to be in God's presence through the disciplines: "Communion becomes transformative when it becomes a regular rhythm of our lives. . . . Communion is coming to God for the sake of God: for his beauty, his love, his presence, his joy. But transformation slips in through the backdoor and comes in sideways. We are changed indirectly by our enjoyment of God."[2] As we sit with and enjoy Jesus through the spiritual disciples, our own transformation is inevitable.

Spiritual disciplines include reading and meditating on God's Word, prayer and fasting, community with other Christians, corporate worship, silence and solitude, giving, service, confession of sins, journaling, celebration, simplicity, and more. As you think about your own abiding relationship with Jesus, how has God used spiritual disciples in your life to draw you to himself? What disciplines is he inviting you to embrace and cultivate to enjoy a more abundant life with him?

A multitude of helpful books have been written on the spiritual disciples. Four books you might consider reading are *Celebration of Discipline* by Richard Foster, *Spiritual Disciples for the Christian Life* by Donald S.

Whitney, *Recapturing the Wonder* by Mike Cosper, and *The Possibility of Prayer* by John Starke.

BE BEFORE YOU DO

In a course like this, it's easy to get excited about the global mission God has given his church. In our excitement, however, there is a temptation to run too quickly into activity, pouring our lives out for others without developing healthy rhythms of abiding with God. Remember that God's calling is for the gospel to renew our own hearts as well as bring renewal to the world. We must not separate the two. In order for us to be effective in reaching others with the gospel, we desperately need to experience our own need for God and rely on him daily.

Hear me clearly: we do need to pour our lives out for God and others. But this must not be through our own might, and not to the detriment of our own souls. Too often as sinful and broken people, we rely on our own strength to serve others rather than serving out of the overflow of our growing life with God. The life God has called us to is a life both fully given to him *and* fully dependent on him. He has called us to a life centered on knowing and enjoying him. Our ministries must flow out of this life of enjoyment.

Jesus knew our tendency to run to work and self-effort. Luke 10:38–42 tells a beautiful story of the necessity of being with Jesus.

> Now as they went on their way, Jesus entered a village. And a woman named Martha welcomed him into her house. And she had a sister called Mary, who sat at the Lord's feet and listened to his teaching. But Martha was distracted with much serving. And she went up to him and said, "Lord, do you not care that my sister has left me to serve alone? Tell her then to help me." But the Lord answered her, "Martha, Martha, you are anxious and troubled about many things, but one thing is necessary. Mary has chosen the good portion, which will not be taken away from her." (Luke 10:38–42)

Jesus was not telling Martha never to serve others. Jesus was teaching Martha (and all of us) that our being *with* Jesus is of greater importance than service *for* Jesus. Both are needed, but it's important to slow down enough to sit at the feet of Jesus, soak in his presence and the life he gives, and then serve others out of his life-giving presence.

Another essential teaching from Jesus is found in John 15:4–5: "Abide in me, and I in you. As the branch cannot bear fruit by itself, unless it abides in the vine, neither can you, unless you abide in me. I am the vine; you are the branches. Whoever abides in me and I in him, he it is that bears much fruit, for apart from me you can do nothing." Here Jesus is teaching the same idea. Just as a branch cannot live—much less bear fruit—apart from the vine, neither can we bear fruit as people on mission unless we abide with Jesus. In fact, if we do not develop regular rhythms of cultivating our lives with Jesus, the end result will be a shallow faith and eventual burnout in our ministry lives.

The lesson is to not put the cart before the horse. Living as one sent on mission is vital as a follower of Jesus, but it is not primary. Being with Jesus is primary. Rather than being constantly busy with being on mission, we need to slow down enough to enjoy our relationship with God and hold this as our most important role in life. As we learn to cultivate our life with God, we remember (and even learn to revel in) our own finiteness and God's infinite power. The mission God calls us to is *his* work, and he delights to use us in expanding his kingdom. We need to remember, however, that this glorious kingdom expansion begins in own hearts.

Jesus himself models this well. In some of his busiest seasons of ministry, Jesus created space in his life to be alone with his Father. Jesus longed to be with God, and this time of communion and solitude with his Father fueled his Spirit-filled life. The night before Jesus chooses the twelve disciples, he sought deep communion with his Father. "In these days he went out to the mountain to pray, and all night he continued in prayer to God. And when day came, he called his disciples and chose from them twelve . . ." (Luke 6:12–13).

The needs of the world will always be pressing in on us. Billions of people have not heard the gospel. Cities and towns around the world have no church and no Bible in their language. People groups in every corner of the world need to hear and experience the gospel message. The world needs to experience the real and everlasting life that only comes through Jesus. If we let need and activity drive our lives and not communion, we will soon realize that we're living life in a way God did not intend. Our calling as followers of Jesus is to pour out our lives for others as we commune with God and are renewed in him daily.

REFLECT

Take a moment to think about a time when you truly felt you relied on God in a situation or season of life. How did your dependence on God, and your communion with him, make a difference? What did God teach you through that experience? Write down some responses, and be ready to share some of what you've written when your group meets.

Also, practice this article's teaching by taking some unhurried time now to enjoy communion with God. Take at least fifteen minutes to practice the spiritual disciples of prayer and reflection (also known as Christian meditation). Consider starting with a few minutes of silence, calming your heart, and asking God to meet you in the quiet. Ask him to grow your abiding life with him. Ask him to meet you in this moment and give you a growing passion to be in his presence. Be prepared to tell your group about your prayer time too.

5

CHURCH ON MISSION

It is not so much the case that God has a mission for his church in the world but that God has a church for his mission in the world. Mission was not made for the church; the church was made for mission—God's mission.
—Christopher J. H. Wright[1]

BIG IDEA

Christians are called to root their lives in a relationship with God, share the gospel with others, multiply disciples, and help start and strengthen new churches. God has a significant role for you to play in his mission. As you work through this lesson, pray that the Holy Spirit would work in your heart to bring conviction and direct you to your place in God's global mission.

OPENING ACTIVITIES

Gather in your cohort or group and discuss your responses to the article, "Abide with God." What have you learned from times in your life when you felt you truly relied on God? What was your experience like when you took time to pray and reflect at the end of the article?

In this lesson, we are going to talk about the mission of the church. As a cohort or group, write down your collective thoughts to the following questions. We will come back to them at the end of the lesson to see how these thoughts have changed or grown.

- What is the mission of the church? (What is the church, and therefore local churches, called to be and do in the world?)
- How has God called individual Christians to participate in this mission?

LESSON

This session's lesson will examine the mission of the church and its key activities in the world. At points during this lesson, you may need to consult the following list. A disciple is someone who . . .

- Walks intimately with Jesus
- Not only soaks in the teaching of Jesus but adopts his character and way of life
- Becomes so much like their master Jesus that they remind others of him
- Makes new disciples

Questions: Which of these discipleship traits is most challenging for you? How do you think God is calling you to grow in this area?

Read about three incidents in the founding of the church in Philippi:

- Lydia's conversion (Acts 16:11–15)
- The jailer's conversion (Acts 16:25–34)
- The church started (Acts 16:40)

Question: For each passage, how do you see God growing and establishing his church at this point in the story?

HEART QUESTIONS

The mission God has given his church is to abide with him, grow to be like him, worship in community with others, and make his glory known to the world through evangelism, discipleship, and church planting. What do each of these areas look like in your life?

How are you sharing the gospel and discipling others in your life right now? Or if you aren't, what is keeping you from being faithful in these areas?

What might God be calling you to do as a result of this lesson?

RENEWAL IN THE GOSPEL

Throughout this course, as you learn together with others, it's good to pay attention to the things that are stirred up in your own heart individually. This week's lesson potentially raises a unique set of concerns. Why? *Because "doing church" with sinful people is complicated.* Many of us have at times been hurt at church, disappointed by people, or frustrated by leadership. We have personal history that complicates the way we think about the church as an institution.

And if this hasn't been your own experience, it is for people you know.

Do you have anything to talk to the Lord about in this regard? Are there any "open wounds"—or "old scabs"—that affect your ability to think about doing mission as part of a church community? Have you had joy in being part of the Lord's church? Do you need the Lord to give you courage to be a part of the church, with its broken people, going forward?

Tell the Lord what's in your heart, writing briefly about it. When your group is ready, share some of what you wrote if you are comfortable doing so.

GROUP PRAYER

Consider each of the four key calls we discussed today. Pray through ways you need God to grow you in each of these areas, remembering that they are not separate or distinct calls but are connected in our lives and work.

- Abide with God and worship him.
- Share Jesus with others.
- Make and multiply disciples.
- Start healthy churches.

PREPARING FOR THE NEXT LESSON

Read and reflect. On your own, before the next time your group meets, read the article "You Were Created to Live Sent," which comes next in this book. Also answer the question at the end of that article, and be prepared to share your answer at the next meeting. **Allow at least 30 minutes for this preparation.**

Memorize. If your class is memorizing Scripture, learn John 15:4–5.

> "Abide in me, and I in you. As the branch cannot bear fruit by itself, unless it abides in the vine, neither can you, unless you abide in me. I am the vine; you are the branches. Whoever abides in me and I in him, he it is that bears much fruit, for apart from me you can do nothing."

Activity. If your leader assigns this activity or if it sounds helpful to you, open up your home and be hospitable to your neighbors or non-Christian friends in the coming weeks. Cook them a good meal, share stories, and love them well. Look for ways to share Jesus by your words and actions.

FURTHER RESOURCES

» *A Praying Life* by Paul Miller
» *Theology and Practice of Mission* edited by Bruce Ashford
» *Global Church Planting* by Craig Ott and Gene Wilson
» *Total Church* by Tim Chester and Steve Timmis

Lesson

ARTICLE

YOU WERE CREATED TO LIVE SENT

To prepare for LESSON 6, read this article ahead of time and answer the questions that follow.

Identity can be a tricky thing. We can find our identity in being a son or daughter, a parent, a teacher, a businessman, or a barista. The list goes on. As Christians, however, our primary identity is found in Christ. We are first and foremost children of God. Everything else in life should be shaped by this identity. Sadly, finding our identity in Christ alone is easier said than done. At least, it was for me.

My whole Christian life, I longed to be a cross-cultural missionary. For several years, I had the opportunity to learn a language and culture, share the gospel, and make disciples in Kathmandu, Nepal. It was truly a dream come true. After years of preparation and planning, I was finally doing ministry in a cross-cultural setting. It shaped me in ways that few things have.

Over time, I found a lot of my identity in being a missionary—too much, in fact. Without me realizing it, it took over as the main part of my identity. I wore it like a badge of honor. I talked about it, wrote about it, and made sure people knew I was a missionary. Even while I was back in the United States to get married, I made sure people knew we were only in the US for a short time. However, the Lord had other plans. Instead of going back overseas as a newly married couple, we were led to stay and help send others to the field from our local church.

It was a painful season of discouragement. If I wasn't a cross-cultural missionary, who was I? I had made being a missionary core to my identity, rather than Christ being the core. I made being a missionary an idol, and when it was taken from me, I was crushed.

WE ARE CREATED TO LIVE SENT

During this season of wrestling with my identity, I asked the question: *Who am I if I'm not a missionary?* This question led me to realize that my understanding of missions was wrong. For so long, I understood a calling to missions as it related to place and position. Where should you be? What position should you hold? But although location is important, it is secondary. Identity is primary. The primary question about calling is not where you are, what position you hold, or what specific work you are doing. The question is *whose* you are. It is your identity in Christ that matters most.

My identity and purpose had not changed; only my location changed. I was no longer a cross-cultural missionary in Nepal, but that did not mean I was no longer called to live on mission. I was still called to share Jesus and make disciples. Mission is primarily about our identity in Christ because God's mission begins in our hearts and extends outward to the world. Our activity and location are simply details in the grand narrative of that story.

When we make missions primarily about location and position, we can easily see ourselves as employees of God. But God's calling to us is far greater than that of a corporation or employer. He doesn't just give us a job to do, he adopts us into his family and gives us all of the riches of Christ. In this way, we aren't just sent ones, we're *beloved* sent ones. We are family, deeply loved and sent out on mission to make God's love known.

Jesus teaches this in John 20:19–22 when he meets his disciples after his resurrection: "Jesus came and stood among them and said to them, 'Peace be with you.' When he had said this, he showed them his hands and his side. Then the disciples were glad when they saw the Lord. Jesus said to them again, 'Peace be with you. As the Father has sent me, even so I am sending you.' And when he had said this, he breathed on them and said to them, 'Receive the Holy Spirit.'"

Here we see Jesus giving words of comfort. He starts by blessing the disciples, saying, "Peace be with you," and showing evidence of his resurrection. After the disciples rejoice at being reunited with their Lord, Jesus then sends them out on mission to the world with the blessing of peace and the gift of the Holy Spirit's presence.

In this passage, Jesus was speaking directly to his disciples, the apostles whom God would use to establish and lead the early church. Although Jesus was directly speaking to these men, the call to be witness is not just for the disciples but for every Christian. Jesus sends us out on mission just as he was sent, as one loved by God and empowered to make that same love known to all nations. Every Christian, no matter what their personality, occupation, or location is sent with the gospel into the world.

At times in my ministry, I've mentored people who struggle with this idea. They doubt whether the call to share the gospel and make disciples is for every Christian. They wonder if they too are called and empowered to make Jesus known to the world around them. It's a good question and one worth considering. Are all Christians called to live on mission?

Let's look back to the end of the Great Commission in Matthew 28:20. Here Jesus gives us a promise that we often overlook, the promise of his presence. "And behold, I am with you always, to the end of the age." At the end of Jesus's command to take the gospel out, he promises that he will be with us to the very end. Jesus promises to be with his people, as they live on mission, till he returns again. The implication here is that the commission to make disciples of all nations applies to the followers of Jesus until he returns, long past the time of the apostles and the early church.

Second, the call to live on mission is not an isolated call in just a few places in Scripture, but a clear theme of the New Testament. The Scriptures provide a convincing apologetic that those who follow Jesus are his witnesses. Jesus himself, in his powerful Sermon on the Mount in Matthew 5:13–16, urges the thousands listening to be his gospel witnesses to a watching world.

> "You are the salt of the earth, but if salt has lost its taste, how shall its saltiness be restored? It is no longer good for

anything except to be thrown out and trampled under people's feet. You are the light of the world. A city set on a hill cannot be hidden. Nor do people light a lamp and put it under a basket, but on a stand, and it gives light to all in the house. In the same way, let your light shine before others, so that they may see your good works and give glory to your Father who is in heaven."

The apostle Peter in 1 Peter 2:9 tells his readers they are God's chosen people, called to make the glory of God known. "But you are a chosen race, a royal priesthood, a holy nation, a people for his own possession, that you may proclaim the excellencies of him who called you out of darkness into his marvelous light." Later in his letter (3:15), Peter urges those who suffer persecution for their faith to "always [be] prepared to make a defense to anyone who asks you for a reason for the hope that is in you." Peter's was speaking to normal everyday Christians seeking to live faithfully in their culture and context, people like you and me.

We can also look at the unfolding theme of the book of Acts as evidence of God's desire for the church as a whole to make and multiply disciples. From Jesus's call to his disciples in Acts 1:8 to be his witness in Jerusalem and beyond, to the Spirit's empowering presence with God's global people in Acts 2, to the movement of the gospel through God's people, including Paul, Timothy, and others, all of these movements in Acts point to a church on the move. It wasn't simply pastors and missionaries doing mission, but the whole people of God living out the gospel in word and deed, making an impact wherever they went.

John 20:19–20 and Matthew 28:18–20 are not the only Scripture passages that communicate this reality of being sent out with the gospel. Each of the Gospels and the book of Acts contains a Great Commission passage that complements John 20 and urges those who follow Jesus to be his witnesses in the world (Mark 16:15–16; Luke 24:47; Acts 1:8). These passages, when understood together, along with the work of Paul and other early missionaries found in the New Testament, give a clear and compelling missiological apologetic to share Jesus, make and multiply disciples, and plant new churches. But the work of being a witness sent out into the world is more than a command, it is a new identity rooted in the person and work of Jesus.

At its core, Jesus is teaching that mission is more than activity. Our mission is rooted in the person of God. Before the creation of the world, our triune God had a plan to redeem the world from the death it would experience. The Father, in union with the Son and the Spirit, sent the Son into the world to redeem it. The Father and Son then sent the Spirit to bring conviction of sin and provide life to the church. Finally, the Father, Son, and Holy Spirit (the triune God) sent the church—you and me—out on mission to the world. My point is that mission is more than just activity, it's identity. We don't simply do the work of witnessing, we *are* witnesses!

REFLECT

Take time to reflect, pray, and write down some responses to the following questions. Be ready to share some of your thoughts when your group meets.

How does rooting your evangelism and discipleship of others in identity over mere activity change the way you think about sharing your faith with others?

What experiences and accompanying emotions, positive or negative, do you have about sharing your faith? How can you bring these experiences and emotions to the Lord and ask him to both renew you and empower you for mission?

6

LIVING SENT

Christian disciples are sent men and women—sent out in the same work of world evangelism to which the Lord was sent, and for which he gave his life. Evangelism is not an optional accessory to our life. It is the heartbeat of all that we are called to be and do.
—Robert E. Coleman[1]

BIG IDEA

Every follower of Christ has an important role to play in seeing the kingdom of God expand around the world. The question is, what role do you play? This session will lay a theological foundation and provide practical tools to share Jesus and make disciples wherever you find yourself.

OPENING ACTIVITY

This week we are going to talk more about living our lives on mission and sharing Jesus with others. As you think about your own life, consider the following:

- What experiences and accompanying emotions, positive or negative, do you have about sharing your faith?

- How can you more practically live on mission in your everyday life? What barriers or internal struggles do you need to overcome to make Jesus known to others?

Gather as a cohort, or in pairs, and have each person share their responses.

LESSON

This session's lesson is about living as a person who is sent as a witness to the good news of Jesus's life, death, and resurrection. During the lesson, read the following testimonies of Christians living on mission in their everyday lives and consult the questions that follow.

College Student

"While I was a student in college, the Lord taught me so much about living sent in the season and station that he placed me in. In his sovereignty, he prepared my comings and goings. I would pray often that God would first give me the desire to serve my classmates and those around me, as well as for opportunities to do so. God provided by allowing me to slow down and see that I could help my classmates with everyday needs. Meeting for coffee or buying them lunch when they were suffering, helping a friend who is blind navigate the way to our classroom each week, or meeting up with a group of classmates to study together are just a few examples. Through jumping in on their rhythms of life and meeting practical needs, I had many opportunities to share the gospel—the truth that God loves them and that Jesus is the way, the truth, and the life."

Stay-at-Home Mom

"I was once a cross-cultural missionary and now am a stay-at-home mom with two little kids. I am busy and have very little bandwidth. It would be easy for me to stay at home and only get out when it's absolutely necessary. Thankfully, very early on, I realized the need to live on mission even when life is busy. I looked at my life and found a place where my rhythms of being a mom could intersect with the lives of unbelievers. I now take my kids to the local library for their weekly story time. While at the library, I seek to make real friendships with the moms there. Two of the other moms have become my good friends and I've shared the gospel with them on a regular basis. One of these ladies and her family now come to my church and attend our small group. They seem close to following Jesus. I'm beginning to realize that evangelism is not a program or a position but a regular rhythm of life that I can do today and every day."

Office Worker

"Every day I work alongside several dozen men and women who do not know Jesus. These are people that I see around the office, chat with on breaks, and get to know slowly over time. These are my people. As I began to be discipled and grow in my faith, I realized that God had placed me in this office to demonstrate and declare the gospel. Over the last few months, I have become intentional with my conversations. I've started a small Bible study with a few coworkers, and I'm even hosting the office staff party in my home this Christmas. I'm praying God gives me even more chances to share my faith!"

What themes or patterns do you notice from these stories of people living their life on mission?

What potential barriers are these people having to overcome to make Jesus known?

From these examples, what could you apply to your own life?

Later in the lesson, you will need to consult the following Gospel Map diagram.[2]

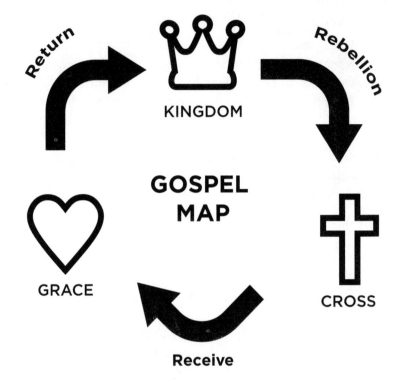

KINGDOM

**GOSPEL
MAP**

GRACE

CROSS

Receive

HEART QUESTIONS

What are the most challenging areas for you when it comes to living sent (sharing Jesus with others)? For example, consider your own walk with God, your misperceptions about evangelism, how you structure your life, how you are in relationships, and what you talk about with others.

What practical steps can you take to live sent in your everyday life?

RENEWAL IN THE GOSPEL

Living missionally can be, when we experience it, quite exhilarating. But often those are irregular flashes of enjoyment rather than a consistent way of life. Many followers of Jesus long for more. Given the idea that they could experience more freedom in their walk with Christ and in their interactions with other people, they respond with a bit of excitement—*I would love to be more like that!* The idea hovers out on the horizon as a tantalizing possibility. Perhaps you can think of someone you know who seems blessedly *unselfconscious*—who loves people and seems not to worry about what anyone thinks of them. That way of life is deeply attractive. Take a moment to reflect and write about these questions:

- When have you experienced something of the joy and freedom of living out your identity as a beloved sent one?

- Does this normally happen in your life? If not, what robs you of this freedom? What are the obstacles to missional living in your heart?

When your group is ready, share some of what you wrote if you are comfortable doing so.

GROUP PRAYER

- Pray about the areas in your life where you could most grow in living sent.
- Pray for a deeper knowledge and understanding of your need for God and the greatness of his provision in Christ. Pray that as you grow in the gospel, you would be driven outward toward others in love.

PREPARING FOR THE NEXT LESSON

Read and reflect. On your own, before the next time your group meets, read the article "Crossing Cultures Effectively," which comes next in this book. Also answer the questions at the end of that article, and be prepared to share your answers at the next meeting. **Allow at least 30 minutes for this preparation.**

Memorize. If your class is memorizing Scripture, learn 1 Corinthians 15:3–4.

> For I delivered to you as of first importance what I also received: that Christ died for our sins in accordance with the Scriptures, that he was buried, that he was raised on the third day in accordance with the Scriptures.

Activity. You just practiced sharing the gospel—so don't stop now. Make sharing Jesus in word and deed an everyday part of your life. Here are two practical next steps:

1. Think of one area of life you can adjust to be more intentional with the gospel. What rhythm of life can you change to make Jesus known to others? Take steps to begin to change this rhythm of life in the coming week.

2. Share the Gospel Map with someone else before you come back to class. Remember, you can simply use it as a guide to tell the gospel story. Be ready to talk about your experiences next week.

FURTHER RESOURCES

» *Tell the Truth* by Will Metzger

» *Tradecraft* by Caleb Crider, Larry E. McCrary, Rodney Calfee, and Wade Stephens

» *The Gospel Comes with a House Key* by Rosaria Butterfield

» *The Mission-Centered Life* by Bethany Ferguson

CROSSING CULTURES EFFECTIVELY

To prepare for LESSON 7, read this article ahead of time and answer the questions that follow.

My final semester of college had just finished and it was time to apply what I had been learning. For three and a half years I had read books and sat in classes on culture, missionary practices, anthropology, and a host of other things that were preparing me for this moment—being a cross-cultural missionary. For my final semester, I had taken an internship in Beijing, China, so that I could work under an established missionary. It was an amazing opportunity to shadow a man who worked hand-in-hand with Christians in the persecuted Chinese church. What my time of training didn't prepare me for was the little old lady who cut me off in line.

There I was, ordering food at a McDonald's in Beijing, an appropriate distance from the person in front of me, when this little old grandmother wedged her body between me and the register and proceeded to order. I thought, *What are you doing, lady?* I looked at her with unkind eyes and said even more unkind things to myself. She just cut right in front of me where no space existed! As my anger grew, I began to take stock of my surroundings. I was the only person ordering food who was trying to stand in line. Everyone else just rushed to the front in some sort of ordered chaos. I asked myself, *Was the lady being rude or was she just following a cultural order I didn't understand?* What I interpreted as wrong behavior was really just different. In fact, maybe I was the one being rude.

This simple experience (repeated many times in different ways) taught me that understanding, interpreting, and being able to navigate culture effectively is a valuable missionary skill, one of the most foundational of all cross-cultural missionary skills. In fact, it is so core to being a cross-cultural missionary that it's even in the name: *cross-cultural.*

Simply put, culture is at the core of ministry. Actually, culture is at the core of human life.

Learning to cross cultures effectively is not an easy task, but it's one of the main skills needed to do ministry well. Whether you want to share Jesus and make disciples in your neighborhood, across town, or around the world, understanding and being able to navigate culture is a necessary skill.

In this week's lesson we will learn more about what culture is, why it matters, and how to move forward as a cultural learner. Take time now to read through the following three cultural concepts. If you understand these well, they can help you navigate crossing culture in life and in ministry. Although there are other cultural concepts you might also need to understand depending on your context, these three provide a good base for understanding cultural differences.

HOT VS. COLD CLIMATE (RELATIONSHIP VS. TASK)

Breaking cultural understanding into the two simple categories of "hot" and "cold" climates is helpful. Almost every culture in the world falls into one of these two categories. Hot climate refers to cultures that are relationship-based and cold climate refers to cultures that are task-based.

Like the names imply, these cultures roughly fall along the lines of the geographical climates they are in. For example, Latin cultures are often hot climates or relationship-based. Latin cultures place a high value on relationships over tasks. This does not mean they devalue tasks, but that things happen best through relationships.

Germany or Scandinavia would be an example of a cold-climate culture. Tasks and being efficient are seen as high priorities. Again, relationships are also valuable in a cold-climate culture; they are just approached differently.

This broad level of cultural understanding, though it may seem simple, can be very helpful in building relationships with people from different cultures once you understand it.

It's important for us to remember that one culture or cultural norm is not better than another. Cultures are simply different. Every culture has strengths and limitations. Every culture reflects the beauty and creativity of God and the cultural mandate he has given his people.

The next two cultural concepts also will often fall along the same lines of hot and cold climate, though not always.

TIME VS. EVENT

Are you wearing a watch? Does your phone constantly display a clock? Did you feel rushed to get out of your house this morning? Do you have a meeting or a place you need to be at a certain time today? If you answered yes to one or all of these questions, you probably live in a culture controlled by time. But many places in the majority (non-Western) world, or places that are more agricultural, often value the exactness of time less. If that's where you live, you might value the part of the day more than the exactness of the minute, or people in your culture may value spending time with a good friend even if it means being late for the next meeting.

Understanding how a culture sees and values time is an important concept to grasp. Valuing events or relationships over time isn't bad, but for those in the Western world it can be a difficult concept to grasp.

I remember attending my first Tibetan wedding. I was excited for the cultural experience, but my excitement soon turned to confusion and then anger. The wedding was to start at 2:00 p.m. I arrived at 2:00, a rookie mistake. But I knew I lived in an event-based culture, so when guests started to arrive half an hour late, I was not surprised. However, when the bride arrived more than an hour late and the groom was still not there after three hours, I began reading my culture into the situation: "They don't value their guests" or, "The groom stood the bride up. Oh no. Poor girl." My lack of understanding the difference between time and event cultures ruined my day and caused me a lot of frustration.

If you've spent any time traveling the world, you will notice these differences. Over the years, when I've worked in the US church or served alongside church leaders in Western Europe or in a large global city, time has been a significant factor in how we relate to each other. Our meetings start and finish on time, and we organize our work and relationships based on meetings and our schedules. This may sound like a shallow way of doing relationships, but it doesn't have to be. Time, events, and schedules simply allow people and society to move along well. Relationships can and do flourish in this cultural norm.

My experience in Latin America, Africa, and much of Asia is different. Society and the way people engage in life centers on people and events in their lives—not primarily time. A meeting starts when everyone gets there, not at a certain time. The meeting ends when the business is done, not at the stroke of a clock. The way people move through life is from conversation to conversation and from person to person, not from hour to hour. This doesn't mean hot-climate cultures are not productive or effective; they simply see life as moving along relationship lines.

INDIVIDUAL VS. COLLECTIVE

One of the most identifiable characteristics of being an American like me is our sense of individuality. Scholars have noted that individualism is at the very core of American culture.[3] To be an American is to be an individual and value autonomy. It is a core cultural value.

I remember growing up hearing the mantras of individualism: "You can be whoever you want to be." "You need to stand on your own two feet." Even now as a parent, one of the main reasons I give my children praise is for being independent—when they act and make decisions on their own. Being independent is not a bad thing, and it's a needed value to some degree. However, not everyone in the world values individualism to the extent Americans or others in the West do. Not everyone or every culture values the individual over the group. Other cultures place more of an emphasis on the collective than they do on the individual.

In a collectivistic society people don't make significant decisions on their own. They consult family, friends, and the community at large. To act independently in decision-making would be disrespectful and cause disharmony in the group. A popular Chinese proverb illustrates this point: "You cannot clap with just one hand."

The deep commitment to community is a beautiful value that should be instructive for those coming from an individualistic society. It should be especially instructive for those in the church. As we read and engage with the Bible, we need to remember that the cultures found within its pages were much more collective and community-centric than they were individual-oriented.

The three cultural frameworks mentioned above are just a few of the concepts you can learn, engage with, and appreciate as you seek to cross cultures effectively. Again, when it comes to culture, it is often helpful to see the differences in cultural understanding and practice not as a right or wrong, but simply as different. Stepping into these cultural differences with a grace-centered posture of humility and teachability allows you to see the beauty of God in his created people.

REFLECT

How have you seen the cross-cultural concepts above play out in your life and relationships? What value and beauty do you see in each perspective? Try to think about specific examples, and write down some responses. Be ready to share some of your thoughts when your group meets.

7

UNDERSTANDING CULTURE

*God reveals himself through all the cultures of the world and all
the peoples within those cultures. When we see the differences
of others, we may well be seeing more of God. He cannot be
contained in or explained from only one cultural perspective.*
—**Duane Elmer**[1]

BIG IDEA

Everyone has a culture and is shaped by cultural distinctives around
them. In this lesson we will learn what culture is, why it matters, and
how to navigate cultural differences in order to build friendships with
those of other cultures and make the name of Jesus known.

OPENING ACTIVITIES

In your cohort or group, share your thoughts about how you've seen
the three cross-cultural concepts in the article "Crossing Cultures Effectively" play out in your life. (Those concepts were task vs. relationship,
time vs. event, and individual vs. collective.)

Also in your group, read the parable below and discuss the questions
that follow.

A terrible storm stranded a monkey on an island. While waiting for the raging waters to recede, he spotted a fish struggling to swim against the current. It seemed to the monkey that the fish was having a hard time and needed assistance. Being kind-hearted and filled with compassion, the monkey resolved to help the fish. The monkey found a tree leaning precariously over the spot where the fish seemed to be struggling. At considerable risk to himself, the monkey moved far out on a limb, reached down, and snatched the fish from the raging waters. Fighting his way back to the safety of his shelter, he carefully laid the fish on dry ground. The monkey had risked a lot, but he felt it was worth it to help this fish in need. For a few moments, the fish showed excitement but soon settled into a peaceful rest.

— An Eastern parable[2]

- What was the motivation behind the monkey's actions?[3]
- What did the monkey assume about the fish's struggle, context, and needs?
- What can we learn from this parable about crossing cultures to share the gospel?

LESSON

This session's lesson will be about understanding cultures. During the lesson, you may be asked to refer to the following sets of questions:

About culture:

- What are some cultural features of (1) your country, (2) your region, and (3) your family?
- Which of these cultural distinctives have especially shaped you?
- How might these cultural distinctives vie for your allegiance to the culture of Christ's kingdom as expressed in Scripture? Can you think of a specific example from your life, or in the culture of your country, region or family?

About ethnocentrism:

- What specific examples of ethnocentrism do you see in your culture and in yourself?

- What are specific ways in which you can push against your ethnocentrism and effectively love those from other cultures and other ways of thinking?

You might also need to read the following case study and discuss the questions that follow it.

Case Study: Trouble Adjusting to a New Culture

Lucas and Ana are a young couple who moved from Brazil to Cairo, Egypt, just eighteen months ago. Their experience so far has been a mixture of highs and lows. They have enjoyed the adventure of moving to a new place and engaging a new culture, but settling down and making Egypt home has been harder than they expected. They have done their best to adapt, including jumping into language learning, taking walks through their neighborhood, meeting their neighbors, serving alongside their mission team, and praying for the city. Although there have been moments of excitement and beauty, they've often felt lost and confused by the culture and people around them. They want to be rooted in the culture and accepted by the people around them, but they feel like outsiders in their community.

People have been very kind and they have even been invited into a few homes for meals. But since the month of Ramadan came, with its practice of fasting from food and drink from dawn till sunset, their interactions with people have dried up. Even when they do go into homes, although people are kind, they are distant and relationships don't seem to go anywhere. The gospel conversations they do have with people are quickly redirected. People have stopped responding to their requests to meet together to study the Bible.

In the past few months, Lucas and Ana have noticed their attitude toward people and situations changing. They used to enjoy the afternoons when they would go out to spend time with people and practice language. This week, talking to people has been extremely hard and they would rather stay home. It's beginning to feel like they will never be able to communicate, and they are tired of feeling incompetent.

Last weekend, they traveled out into the countryside to a friend's wedding. The wedding lasted several days and multiple times they were put into situations where they did not understand what to do or what to say, and were corrected for doing the wrong thing. They were clearly outsiders and felt more alone and incompetent than ever. The last day of the wedding, they pulled away and kept to themselves. They ended the weekend feeling more bitter and critical of their host culture than they had before.

Lucas and Ana feel these changes occurring in their hearts, but they do not know what to do. Their teammates have been on the field much longer and do not seem to struggle with the same things. Lucas and Ana have started to wonder what in the world is happening and just how effective they can be in Egypt. On their worst days they want to stay home, enjoy things from their own culture, and not engage with their host culture or its people.

Discussion: Lucas and Ana are in the midst of culture shock. They want to understand their situation and move toward health, but they don't know what to do. Culture shock has left them disoriented and hurting. Lucas and Ana are some of your good friends and they reach out to you for help and advice. Answer and discuss the following questions:

- What is happening in Lucas and Ana's situation?
- As a friend and part of their support team from their local church, what advice would you give Lucas and Ana?
- How could you practically encourage and support Lucas and Ana in this situation?

HEART QUESTIONS

How have your cultural preferences kept you from loving others well?

What practical steps can you take in your current life to better understand cultures and cross them effectively?

RENEWAL IN THE GOSPEL

Do you like to be right? Crossing cultures requires humility. Moving into a different culture requires us to hold loosely to our ideas about "the right way to do things." This is challenging because for many of us the desire to be right—or to do things rightly—can be quite powerful even in our own cultural context. In those places where you are convinced that you do things "right," it's easy to be ungracious toward those who, by comparison, don't!

Think of your attitude toward other drivers, for instance. Do you believe you're a better driver than a lot of people? Are you exasperated by the things they do or don't do behind the wheel? Or, do you get frustrated by other people's poor use of the English language? Do you get riled up by people who whisper in the movie theater, or who come to church late, or who parent their children in ways you don't understand?

You may want to respond, "But using your turn signal isn't a cultural preference; it's just the right thing to do!" But that's the nature of these things. We have a deep conviction that the way we do things is *just right*.

This week, pay attention to areas in which being right is important to you. Ask your spouse or roommate what they think! Right now, take a few minutes to write about these things. You might ask yourself the following questions:

Am I a proud person, and how does this express itself?

Why do I love to be right?

Invite the Holy Spirit to give you insight and the humility to be open to how these things operate in your heart. When your group is ready, share some of what you wrote if you are comfortable doing so.

GROUP PRAYER

Pray for God to grow your curiosity about the cultural preferences of others, and to help you grow in having a learner's heart. Also pray for opportunities to engage with people from other cultures and make friends in your day-to-day life.

PREPARING FOR THE NEXT LESSON

Read and reflect. On your own, before the next time your group meets, read the article "Suffering and the Christian Life," which comes next in this book. Also answer the questions at the end of that article and complete the prayer exercise, and be prepared to share your answers at the next meeting. **Allow at least 45 minutes for this preparation.**

Memorize. If your class is memorizing Scripture, learn Acts 10:34–35.

> So Peter opened his mouth and said: "Truly I understand that God shows no partiality, but in every nation anyone who fears him and does what is right is acceptable to him."

Activity. Stories are often the best place to see the cultural values and distinctives of a given culture. Choose a country, ethnic group, or distinct culture that interests you and engage in some of their stories. Consider doing one of the following:

- Read a children's book or fairy tale from that culture.

- Read a novel written by a person from that culture, set in their homeland.
- Watch a foreign-language film set within the culture.

As you read or watch these stories, what cultural values and distinctives do you observe?

FURTHER RESOURCES

» *Cross-Cultural Connections* by Duane Elmer

» *Foreign to Familiar* by Sarah Lanier

» *Ministering Cross-Culturally* by Sherwood Lingenfelter and Marvin Mayers

» *The 3D Gospel: Ministry in Guilt, Shame, and Fear Cultures* by Jayson Georges

7

SUFFERING AND THE CHRISTIAN LIFE

To prepare for LESSON 8, read this article ahead of time and answer the questions that follow.

NOTE: The story that follows tells of the brutal murder of Christian missionaries. If you don't wish to read the details of such an account, skip ahead to the fourth paragraph below.

The sun was setting in the small Indian village of Manoharpur when missionary Graham Stains and his two sons Philip and Timothy, age ten and seven, decided they would sleep in the jeep outside a local church after a long day of ministry.[4] The boys were on break from school and had joined their dad as he set up a medical camp and did ministry among the leper community. As Graham and his boys settled in for the night, they were unaware that an angry mob of fifty Hindu extremists were headed their way, determined to teach the missionary a lesson.

Graham Staines was an Australian medical missionary who spent thirty-four years serving the community, focusing primarily on helping those with leprosy and translating the New Testament into the Ho dialect.[5] While serving in India, he met his wife, also a single missionary, and they started a family. Graham was known and beloved in the community, but not by all. Many of those who held to an extreme view of Hinduism believed that Graham and those at the mission were forcing the poor in the community to convert to Christianity. These wild allegations, that were later proven false, drove the mob to violence.

So, in the cover of night, while Graham and his sons slept, the mob approached the jeep, doused it with gasoline, and lit it on fire. Graham and his sons reportedly tried to escape, but the mob kept them trapped in the jeep and watched them burn to death. Others in the village tried to help but they too were attacked and the village church was burned.[6]

This is a hard story to take in, hard to imagine three people who loved Jesus so much suffer so greatly. But suffering is a reality for those who step out in faith and follow Jesus. In fact, suffering has been a reality for most of the church for most of history. From the early days of the church (Acts 4) to this very day, Christians from around the world and across time have suffered greatly. Open Doors, a ministry that serves the global persecuted church, estimates that nearly five thousand Christians a year die under persecution for their faith in Jesus. Millions more Christians live in places where high levels of persecution and discrimination are common realities.[7]

The Staines family and others who have suffered deeply are more than stories of the past. These are our brothers and sisters in Christ who are personally suffering because they choose to follow Jesus. One of the major themes that comes up over and over again as I have pastored missionaries and befriended national leaders around the world is the truth that *a call to missions is a call to suffer.* When we step out to serve Jesus on the front lines of ministry, especially in a cross-cultural context, suffering and spiritual warfare are sure to become our close companions.

In these moments of pain, we must cling to the encouragement we find in 1 Peter 4:12–14, "Beloved, do not be surprised at the fiery trial when it comes upon you to test you, as though something strange were happening to you. But rejoice insofar as you share Christ's sufferings, that you may also rejoice and be glad when his glory is revealed. If you are insulted for the name of Christ, you are blessed, because the Spirit of glory and of God rests upon you." When we suffer for him, we actually share in the sufferings of Christ. Our suffering for his name brings glory to God and brings blessing upon us. It seems crazy to talk about suffering in a positive light, but Jesus himself spoke about such things, preparing his followers for the trials that were sure to come.

Jesus closes the Beatitudes by saying, "Blessed are those who are persecuted for righteousness' sake, for theirs is the kingdom of heaven. Blessed are you when others revile you and persecute you and utter all kinds of evil against you falsely on my account. Rejoice and be glad, for your reward is great in heaven" (Matthew 5:10–12).

Not every Christian will experience persecution as a direct result of being a Christian, but suffering is a promise for every believer. A gospel message devoid of suffering is a gospel message that does not see Christ or his church clearly. If we are to truly follow Jesus, to grow to be like him and make an impact in this world, we need a robust theology of suffering. Paul Borthwick and Dave Ripper write, "Suffering finds us all. Every last one of us. Its forms are varied, numerous, and unique as the very people on earth who experience its consequences. There is no getting around the reality that to be alive is to experience suffering."[8]

Friends, I know that suffering and pain are terrifying concepts to embrace. But developing a theology of suffering is an essential part of the Christian life and even more vital for those living on mission for Jesus. If we want to follow Jesus and live on mission for him, we must be prepared to face increased spiritual warfare, endure hardship, and even suffer for the joy of being found in him and being on mission with him.

Nate Saint, one of five missionaries martyred in the jungles of Ecuador, wrote in his journal before he died, "If we are going to emulate our Savior, we have to identify with the people to whom we take his good news. I don't advocate that we look for suffering; life brings enough of it on its own. But what I do advocate is that suffering is an important prerequisite to ministering to hurting people."[9]

Elisabeth Elliot, one of the missionaries who served alongside Nate Saint, was one who knew suffering well. She both experienced it and wrote about it. In her book *Suffering Is Never for Nothing* she wrote, "Whatever is in the cup that God is offering to me, whether it be pain and sorrow and suffering and grief along with the many more joys, I'm willing to take it because I trust Him."[10]

These are powerful words—not easy, but words for us to meditate on and apply to our own lives. When we suffer in this life, may we be reminded that we belong to the one who suffered beyond measure and who promises us an eternal home where suffering, sin, and death are no more. As we suffer, may we remember that Jesus has promised to be with us in our suffering. He will not abandon us or leave us to suffer alone, but invites us to find rest and comfort him.

REFLECT

Take time to reflect and write down some responses to the following questions. Be ready to share some of your thoughts when your group meets.

Think of a time you have suffered deeply. How did you experience God in the midst of your pain?

As you think about living your life on mission for Jesus, what fears or concerns do you carry?

Lesson

STATE OF THE WORLD

*The church is not meant to call men and women out of the
world into a safe religious enclave but to call them out in order
to send them back as agents of God's kingship.*
—Lesslie Newbigin[1]

BIG IDEA

We live in a big world—a world in need of Jesus. This lesson will take
you on a journey to understand both the vast lostness of our world and
how God is on the move, redeeming his people from every corner of
the earth.

OPENING ACTIVITIES

In your group or cohort, briefly share some of your answers from the
article, "Suffering and the Christian Life." How has God worked in the
midst of suffering in your life? What fears do you have about living on
mission for Jesus?

You may also hear from a visiting cross-cultural missionary today. Please
feel free to ask questions or follow up with the missionary after class.

LESSON

This session's lesson will explore the size of the missionary task before
us and ways God is moving to accomplish it.

HEART QUESTIONS

How are you impacted by the magnitude of lostness in the world and the advance of the gospel in the past century? Are you encouraged or discouraged? Energized or overwhelmed? Joyful or sorrowful? Explain.

RENEWAL IN THE GOSPEL

Matthew's gospel gives us an amazing glimpse into Jesus's response to the often-overwhelming needs of the people he moved among: "When he saw the crowds, he had compassion for them, because they were harassed and helpless, like sheep without a shepherd" (Matthew 9:36). This is the heart of the Lord *today*, too, in response to the staggering needs of Istanbul and Karachi, of Jakarta and Rio de Janeiro. And part of following Jesus is following him into a world broken by sin and suffering. When we follow Jesus, we take up the call to love a world in need of him.

Jesus said, "Blessed are those who mourn" (Matthew 5:4). Though the Christian life is characterized by joy, oddly it's also characterized by sorrow and mourning—as was the life of Jesus, the "man of sorrows." Learning to mourn is part of being moved out in love and mission.

But we shrink from mourning and sadness. Self-protectively, we're drawn to various kinds of "anesthesia" that numb us and to entertainment that distracts us from the world's great need. In order to be sent into a needy world, we need the Holy Spirit to work compassion in our hearts, a compassion that refuses to turn away from people's need.

Reflect on this now in your own life. How has the Lord led you to mourn? How has he stirred compassion in you? How do you shrink back from engaging the world's great need of him? Write down some thoughts, and when your group is ready, share some of what you wrote if you are comfortable doing so.

GROUP PRAYER

Pray for God to open your heart to the urgent need for the gospel to go out. Pray also for God to show you ways he could use you to meet the need for the gospel personally (in your own life), locally (where you are now), and globally (where you may someday go).

PREPARING FOR THE NEXT LESSON

Read and reflect. On your own, before the next time your group meets, read the article "Who Can Be a Missionary?" which comes next in this book. Also answer the questions at the end of that article, and be prepared to share your answers at the next meeting. **Allow at least 30 minutes for this preparation.**

Memorize. If your class is memorizing Scripture, learn John 10:14–16.

> "I am the good shepherd. I know my own and my own know me, just as the Father knows me and I know the Father; and I lay down my life for the sheep. And I have other sheep that are not of this fold. I must bring them also, and they will listen to my voice. So there will be one flock, one shepherd."

Activity. If your leader assigns it or if it sounds helpful to you, take time to reflect on this question: How could you invest your life in seeing the nations come to know and worship Jesus? Give yourself time and space to pray, journal, or talk through this question with a friend.

FURTHER RESOURCES

» *Operation World* by Jason Mandryk

» *Kingdom Without Borders* by Miriam Adeney

» *The Future of the Global Church* by Patrick Johnstone

» *Why Cities Matter* by Stephen Um and Justin Buzzard

Lesson

ARTICLE

WHO CAN BE A MISSIONARY?

To prepare for LESSON 9, read this article ahead of time and answer the questions that follow.

It was a Friday at the church office, often a slow day as many of our staff take the day off to rest up for the weekend. I was in the office that day to meet with a young couple who were considering missions. They wanted to meet up to talk more about their next steps.

We sat across from one another and I listened to their story. They had been in our church for a few years and had loved global missions for as long as they could remember. They had been on several short-term mission trips and enjoyed their time. Both the husband and wife were now finishing seminary and had a desire to be long-term missionaries.

As we talked, I started to ask questions about their readiness for cross-cultural missions and their current life on mission. Although they had been at our church for several years, they were still struggling to get plugged in. When I asked about how they served others or when and where they were sharing the gospel, they admitted they were just too busy to be faithful in these areas. I pressed in on some of these concerns, but their responses left more questions than answers. It was clear to me that although global missions was not out of the picture, a lot of growth needed to happen before they could move overseas and be effective in cross-cultural ministry.

After our meeting, as I headed home, I stopped by a local coffee shop. There I saw a young man I knew well. He served weekly in our church and was a committed member of a Bible study in the city. I knew he was actively sharing his faith. In fact, as I walked up to order, I overheard him talking about spiritual things with a coworker.

He was getting off work so we sat down in the coffee shop to catch up. I asked him questions about his life. To no surprise to me, he was actively loving others, serving his neighbors, and praying for his coworkers—several of whom were devout Muslims. I asked him if he had ever considered being a cross-cultural missionary on one of our teams overseas. To my dismay, he assured me he wouldn't make a good missionary—that he didn't have a call to go overseas and he felt he had nothing of substance to offer.

Experiences like these have helped me realize that there is often a misunderstanding about who can and should be a cross-cultural missionary. These misunderstandings tend toward one of two myths. One myth says anyone at all can be a cross-cultural missionary. The other myth says only a select few can be missionaries. The reality is that neither belief is true. What is true is that a call to cross-cultural missions is a call to continued growth and maturity. A call to missions flows from a life that is already on mission for God.

Let's take a closer look at these two myths.

Myth: Anyone can be a cross-cultural missionary. The argument goes that if you have a personal call or a desire, then you can go as a cross-cultural missionary. If God is calling, who could stop you? This thinking undervalues the role of a missionary by saying that qualification, skill, and past behavior have little value and what ultimately matters is a person's desire. As good as this might sound, it's foolish. Being a missionary must be more than desire.

Think about it in terms of other callings or work:

> **Becoming a pastor.** Let's say a young man came to your church leadership and simply said, "You need to make me a pastor because *I feel called.*" What would your leadership say? They would want

to examine him, look at his past behavior, see his qualification and skills, and then make a judgment as to whether this young man is called and qualified to be a pastor. It would be crazy to simply make him a pastor based on his desire alone.

Becoming an engineer. Let's say a young woman goes to an engineering firm and asks for a job. She is able to articulate her love of the work and her short-term experiences in design and production. What kinds of questions will the engineering firm ask? They will examine her résumé and her education, and will talk with people who have seen her work. Again, it would be foolish for this company to hire this young woman simply based on her desire and love of engineering.

Cross-cultural missions is a calling, but it is *more* than a calling. It's a profession, a craft that requires knowledge, character, and skill. One which few are able to do *well*. Only through the grace of God, and the refinement of a person's character and skills and knowledge over a period of time, can a man or woman be ready to live and serve overseas. Cross-cultural missions is not for just anyone—but it is for many. Global missions is for those who root their lives in Jesus, live on mission wherever they find themselves, and are led by the Spirit of God to live that same kind of missional life cross-culturally.

Myth: Only the elite can be missionaries. On the other side is the belief that almost no one is qualified to be a missionary, and that only the spiritually elite are able to live and serve overseas. This belief is often a product of putting missionaries on a pedestal and believing they have a greater calling and character than the rest of us. Missionaries are no better, or worse, than anyone else. They are simply people seeking to love and serve God but who do it cross-culturally.

Instead of thinking in extremes, we need to think of being a missionary like we would most other professions: some are called and gifted to take the gospel cross-culturally, and others are not. This does not make anyone better or worse. Simply put, God has a unique and grace-centered calling for all of our lives. Some are called and gifted for long-term cross-cultural missions and others are gifted for other valuable roles.

The key question here is, how has God gifted, equipped, and called you for his kingdom? More often than not, missions is available for those who desire to serve overseas. If you are considering a life given to God in cross-cultural ministry, consider the following:

1. **Be committed to walking in Christian community with mature people who can help you discern your call and equip you to grow as a disciple.** Your local church is the primary place of ministry discernment, discipleship, and missionary preparation.

2. **Seek to live a life right now that is committed to communion with God, killing sin in your life, and sharing Jesus with others.** If you're not sharing Jesus and making disciples right now, what makes you think you would do it overseas in a different language and culture?

3. **Have a teachable spirit that is able to receive correction and instruction from others.** God often uses the weak things of this world, those on the margins, to do amazing things. Think about Moses, Rahab, Ruth, Jonah, Peter, and so many others. These were seemingly ordinary people whom God used in extraordinary ways. It's also important to remember that these weak, broken people never stayed in the place where they were. They had a deeply rooted life with God and a willingness to mature and grow.

REFLECT

Take time to reflect, pray, and write down some responses to the following questions. Be ready to share some of your thoughts when your group meets.

As you think about your own life and character, what areas is God calling you to grow in to be more effective in life and ministry?

How could God be using your weaknesses in this season of life, teaching you to depend more on him and his strength?

Lesson

9

YOUR PLACE IN GOD'S GLOBAL MISSION

If you love the glory of God, you cannot be indifferent to missions.
—John Piper[1]

BIG IDEA

We all have a role to play in seeing the kingdom of God expand. Because we are all called to live sent in our everyday lives, we need to make it a priority wherever we find ourselves. This session will help you see more specifically how you might answer the call to share Jesus and make disciples both near and far.

OPENING ACTIVITY

Gather as a cohort or small group and share some of your answers to questions at the end of the article, "Who Can Be a Missionary?" How do you think is God calling you to grow in ministry? How is he teaching you to depend more on him?

LESSON

This final lesson will discuss your specific place and calling in missions. It will end by asking you to consider two questions:

- What is your role in God's global mission?

- What is your next step?

TAKING ACTION

Ways to Live Sent

At the end of the lesson, your leader will have a list of opportunities for you to get more involved with missions both locally and globally.

So, What's Next

This activity[2] will help you think more about your own story, your spiritual giftings, and your calling to living on mission both near and far.

Draw the following playing-card symbols on the left side of a paper, from top to bottom: club, heart, spade, diamond. Also draw an X and an arrow. Then, next to each of these six pictures, answer some questions.

 Clubs. List two or three "clubs" that you belong to. They can be actual clubs or just things you enjoy, like "cooking club" or "football fan club."

 Hearts. List two or three things you're most passionate about: helping the poor, discipleship, foster care, music, organic food, etc.

 Spades. List two or three tools God has given you to make an impact on the world. What are you good at? Encouragement, music, evangelism, working with your hands, teaching, listening, etc.

Diamonds. In three or four words, write what you hope to be remembered for as your legacy on earth.

 What is one thing in your life right now that's keeping you from living on mission or moving out on more faithful mission? It might be a sin pattern, debt, a specific fear, etc.

 What is one thing God is calling you to do as a result of this class?

HEART QUESTIONS

As you reflect back on the last nine lessons, how has God used this class to change your heart and your perspective?

What do you sense God is calling you to do as a result of this class? What will be your next step of obedience?

Is God leading you toward a life of sharing Jesus and making disciples cross-culturally?

RENEWAL IN THE GOSPEL

When we think about the future, and especially when we think in terms of individual calling, all sorts of temptations arise. On the one hand, you may have a particular vision for your life that you long to see unfold. In that case, the temptation is to grab the steering wheel of your life tightly with both hands—to try to manage your life and make things happen according to the script your heart is set on. When your heart is firmly set on a particular vision, it can be annoying to hit obstacles or delays, and you might find yourself refusing to hear voices that express hesitations or raise good questions about the wisdom of the path you're on. The thing you desire—even a life on the mission field—can take an outsized importance in your heart and become an idol to you.

On the other hand, thinking about the future might also cause you to be filled with fear. The very real risks of a life given to the service of Christ may cause you to hold back from seriously considering a "road less traveled." Perhaps then safety, security, and success become the idols that control your decision-making.

As you think about your future, where do you think you're vulnerable? What are the dangers to your heart? Ask the Lord to give you insight into your own heart, and ask him to give you grace to entrust your life to him on a daily basis. You might write briefly about this and, when your group is ready, share some of what you wrote if you are comfortable doing so.

Lesson 9: Your Place in God's Global Mission 87

GROUP PRAYER

Pray for each person in your group as they consider their own call to *live sent wherever they find themselves* and what specific ways God would have them participate in expanding his kingdom.

FOLLOW-UP

Activity 1: Take a **spiritual retreat** in the next few weeks to spend time with Jesus, debrief, and explore what God wants to do in you and through you as a result of this course.

- Take two to three hours alone in a place you find refreshing. This can be in a park, on a hike, at a coffee shop, or in your own home.

- Break up this time with a combination of helpful activities and time for silence, reflection, and prayer.

- Either create your own plan or consider doing a few of the following:

  1. Spend large chunks of time in prayer, both talking with God and listening to him.

  2. Go on a long walk to pray and reflect.

  3. Listen to music that helps you reflect and worship.

  4. Read a book of the Bible in one sitting. Instead of studying the text, simply read the book as a whole while asking God to meet you as you read.

  5. Journal your thoughts, reflections, and questions from the *You Are Sent* course.

  6. If one of the topics in *You Are Sent* interested you, buy one of the further resources from that lesson and begin reading during this time.

  7. Meet with a friend or church leader after your spiritual retreat to process both what God is doing in you and what you sense God wants to do through you.

Activity 2: Gather with your group or cohort several weeks after the end of the last class for a **meal in someone's home**. Take time to process together what you have learned and how God has shaped your heart for mission, and to talk through next steps.

FURTHER RESOURCES

» *Mission Smart* by David Frazier
» *On Being a Missionary* by Thomas Hale and Gene Daniels
» *Is God Calling Me?* by Jeff Iorg
» *The Call* by Os Guinness

Upstream Sending is a church-centric international missions organization committed to putting the church in the driver's seat of sending and missions engagement. We partner with churches to help send their people to gospel-needy people and places around the world. We do this through an interdependent relationship with local churches and work with a host of teams, global leaders, and international organizations. If you would like to learn more about Upstream Sending and where your life might intersect with God's global mission, talk with leaders in your local church and then reach out to us. We would love to help you and your church with your journey into global missions.

Serge Grace at the Fray

Serge is a grace-based, international missions organization bringing together mission and spiritual renewal with over 300 missionaries serving in 25 countries around the world. The connection between on-going, personal gospel transformation and equipping in order to move outward into mission that you've studied in *You Are Sent* is at the center of our work at Serge. If you'd like to see where and how we work, explore missions opportunities ranging from short-term trips to career service, or grow deeper in your relationship with God, please visit us at: Serge.org.

LEADER'S NOTES

As you pick up this book, you may be asking yourself, *Why another global missions course?* There are several helpful missions courses out there designed to shape the hearts and minds of God's people for global missions engagement. Even so, I've come to the conviction that local churches need a global missions course focused on awareness, education, and mobilization that is written by a local church, for local churches.

Although I now lead a missions sending organization, for the previous eleven years, I served as the missions pastor of a local church. One of our core endeavors in global missions was to develop missionaries out of our own membership. For many years, our primary way of doing this was to send them through our eight-month, in-house missionary development program. We had found this program to be very fruitful, but when I was honest with myself, it was not accomplishing what we as church leaders really wanted to see happen. Sure, it was producing cross-cultural missionaries who were being faithful overseas, but most often we did this by developing people that were already faithful servant-leaders with an existing passion for missions. We were doing a poor job of taking the average member, one who loved God but had limited exposure to missions, and empowering him/her to be sent locally and globally.

So, after years of creating and running our in-house missionary development program, a program I loved dearly, we shut it down. Why? Because I believed that if we could create an in-house course focused on educating and mobilizing *every* member of our church for global missions, the kingdom impact would be even greater. The book you hold in your hands is the fruit of this vision.

As I began thinking about crafting the course, to my surprise, I was not alone. There were other church leaders who wanted to see something created by the local church for local churches.

Several years ago, I sent out a survey asking missions pastors and leaders what their dream missions course would be if they could create it from scratch. I got back responses across various denominations and church sizes. They each had different opinions but several themes popped up over and over again:

- A course adaptable and flexible for each church's context
- Robust yet accessible enough for every member of the church
- Biblically rooted and theologically rich
- A format that can be used in a classroom, small group, or in one-on-one discipleship
- A course created to do in community with others
- A course focused on global missions but also empowered every member to share Jesus and make disciples in their own context
- Something that drives people to reach the nations and roots that movement in their life with Jesus

After reading the feedback from missions pastors I know and trust, I reached out to Serge and proposed the idea of writing a missions course for local churches. Serge seemed like the obvious choice for helping me create a missions resource. First, they have been a great sending partner to our local church. They have a proven track record of empowering local churches to fulfill the vision God has given to specific local churches. Second, they have significant writing experience. They have created countless books and resources including *Sonship* and *The Gospel-Centered Life*. Finally, and I think most valuable for this project, they are known for doing missions work out of a posture of weakness and value ministry that flows out of communion with God.

PREPARATION

As you prepare to teach *You Are Sent*, make sure to read through the leader section fully before beginning the course. This will give you a better picture of what the course contains and will allow you to make adjustment or additions based on your local church's needs. Many sections have leader instructions that will help you better prepare to host the course. There's also a cross-cultural experience, described on the next page, that will take planning and resources—so you need to begin now. It adds an interactive global missions experience to the course, and will significantly enhance the effectiveness of *You Are Sent*.

Note that lesson 4 calls for you to arrange for a visitor who will share about living on mission locally, and lesson 8 calls for you to arrange for a cross-cultural missionary to visit and speak. Again, your planning should begin now.

Also, I encourage you to gather ahead of time with others leaders in your church to pray for those going through the course. Pray that God would work powerfully in participants, that both their love for God and for others would increase, and that God would lead them toward greater missions engagement locally and globally.

PRAYER

My prayer is that the love and labor we, as a local-church team, have put into this course will bless you and your people. May it shape the minds, skills, and character of those in your church whom God is calling to give their lives, in various ways, to reach the lost with the gospel of Jesus. But not just that, may all our lives and affections be more centered on Jesus as a result of this course. May we fall more in love with the One we seek to proclaim, and may we experience his grace as we serve out of our weakness and dependence on him.

Nathan Sloan

CROSS-CULTURAL EXPERIENCE

You Are Sent is intended to be a transformative experience for people that pushes them to understand God's passion for all nations and their role in God's global mission. The reality, however, is that a nine-lesson course can only do so much. God often uses a multitude of experiences to draw people into his mission and help refine their call.

With this in mind, I recommend including at some point in the course a simple concept I call a *cross-cultural experience*. These one-day, three-day, or week-long experiences are intended to open people's hearts and minds to what God could be calling them to do as it relates to their sent calling. We want people to experience the beauty and tension that comes with engaging people from other cultures. This simple experience of diving headfirst into cross-cultural relationships and ministry can open doors for deeper conversations, missional exploration, and growing discipleship. Although the experiences are limited and cannot be a substitute for ongoing, regular cross-cultural ministry, they can be a great starting place for many people. If we think of cross-cultural missions like the ocean, the first step for most people is not diving into the deepest part but walking along the shore, experiencing the waves on their feet and allowing the beauty of missions to draw them into its depths.

One-day experience. Within the nine-week timeframe, create an international experience for those in the class. Ideally, this would be a service project—perhaps joining a local ministry that works among refugees or international students. If you live in a city, there is a good chance that there are neighborhoods or apartment complexes where refugees or international students live and work. Do some research and see if there are needs you can meet, organizations your class can volunteer with, or a local international church you can serve alongside. Create this one-day experience to both serve internationals and help open the minds, hearts, and hands of those in your *You Are Sent* class. Make sure to take time after the experience to debrief participants. Encourage them toward deeper work among internationals either in your community or in other places.

Three-day experience. If you and your church are looking for a longer, more intensive experience, consider partnering with a church or organization in a large urban area that can help facilitate a three-day cross-cultural experience. This will be more expensive and time consuming, and it will require more planning, but the benefits will be worth the cost.

Short-term trip. You may also consider ending *You Are Sent* with a short-term trip to visit a missionary from your church or a national partner serving cross-culturally. Work ahead of time with your partner to plan a trip that can allow participants to apply the concepts they have learned while serving the vision and mission of your field partner. Ending *You Are Sent* with a longer cross-cultural experience is a wonderful way to apply all the lessons learned from the class, deepen community among participants, and get to see firsthand what God is doing to expand his glory and goodness around the world.

LESSON 1: GOD'S GLOBAL MISSION IN THE OLD TESTAMENT

NOTE ABOUT TEACHING THE LESSONS: This part of the *You Are Sent* course includes a full text of the lecture portion of the class. It is a guide to how you might teach each lesson's concepts. My hope in providing this is to empower any teacher in a church to feel confident they can teach these lessons. Feel free to teach straight from that text or adapt it based on your own study and experience.

The vision of *You Are Sent* is to provide a global missions course that is written by a local church for local churches. This means flexibility is important. Although I encourage you to cover all the major topics in the lesson content below, it's okay to consider what your church needs and then adjust the content to help meet those needs. This may include combining lessons, adding concepts that are valuable to your church, or adding other resources that enhance the missions-development process. You also might draw on your own experiences. If you desire to learn more about a given topic before teaching, you can read the suggested resources at the end of each lesson.

Keep this teaching portion of the lesson between forty-five and sixty minutes. Learning within community is an essential part of *You Are*

Sent, so include plenty of time for people to interact and discuss. If you choose to teach *You Are Sent* in a classroom setting, break the class up into cohorts of five to eight people and assign cohort leaders to facilitate conversation and encourage participants along the way. Or if you teach the course in a small group setting, you might want to break into discussion groups of three to foster deeper connection.

PREPARATION AND INSTRUCTIONS

For this first lesson's opening activity, place large sheets of paper (like those from a large tear-off display board) on the walls around the room, one for each student, clustered according to cohorts. Provide markers at cohort tables. If you're leading *You Are Sent* in a different format, or wish to print out your own questions, adjust the delivery and structure of this activity to fit your group. Student instructions and suggested questions are in the student section of this book.

LEARNING OBJECTIVES

- To see that God's plan for redeeming people from all nations of the earth has been in place from before the beginning of time and spans both the Old and New Testaments
- To see that redeeming people from every nation, tribe, and tongue is at the very heart of God

LESSON CONTENT

Too often when we think about missions and reaching people with the gospel, our conversations start in the New Testament. We may root missions in the Great Commission, in the ministry of Paul, or even in the earthly ministry of Jesus. Although these are essential places to learn and grow in our missions understanding, they are not the best place to start. The place to begin our missions journey is with God himself. He is a missionary God who has a pursuing love for his people among every language, tribe, and nation on earth. Our missionary God wrote a missionary book, the Bible, that unfolds for us a beautiful redemption plan. And it's a plan he is calling you to understand, embrace, and live out.

Although the Bible has many significant themes woven through its pages, none speak as loudly or as foundationally as God's passionate and pursuing love for his people. Sally Lloyd-Jones says it well in her book, the *Jesus Storybook Bible*. She writes that God's love through the gospel is, "God's never stopping, never giving up, unbreaking, always and forever love."[1] That is the beauty of God's love for us and for all nations. It can't be stopped. The love of God, worked out through his plan of redemption, will rescue people from every nation on earth. It's a promise that God himself makes and God himself carries out.

As we walk through the pages of the Bible in this first lesson, we will begin to see that God's plan of redemption for all nations is not plan B. It's his plan A, and it has been all along. From the very beginning, God's plan was to redeem both Jew and Gentile, male and female, black and white and Asian and Latino, American and French and Indian and Ethiopian and Thai. God's love is for all people, and the Bible is a story of God's love fulfilled in sending his Son as Savior and establishing his church on earth to fulfill his mission.

Let's open our Bibles and discover God's glorious redemption plan for all peoples.

Give participants time to read each passage aloud as a large group or in smaller groups, mark the passages in their Bibles, and think through how they fit together to display the redeeming love of God. As the teacher, you should read each text beforehand and make notes on the text and how it fits into God's global mission. Feel free to add your own insights. It may be helpful to have participants bring a physical Bible with them to each meeting so they can open their Bibles and mark the passages studied.

Creation

God created the world perfect in every way, and the pinnacle of God's creation was man and woman. He created them in his image and gave them all they could ever need or want (Genesis 1:27–28). In his goodness, God not only created them and provided for their needs, he gave them himself. He lived in close relationship with them in perfect community. He walked with them and talked with them in perfect love.

Fall

Sadly, their perfect love relationship did not last. It was tainted and broken in an act that forever changed the world.

The enemy, Satan, deceived Adam and Eve, and they rebelled against God. Their perfect love relationship with God was broken, just as our relationship with God is broken today. All hope seemed lost, but through God's mercy, at the very moment of their disobedience, God provided a promise of redemption. As God was passing out judgments to Adam, Eve, and Satan, he promised to send a Savior who would one day liberate God's people (including you and me) from the rule of sin and death.

Genesis 3:15. In this moment of judgment, God promised to send a child who would crush the head of Satan, defeating sin and death. Here is the goodness of God on display: even in the midst of judgment, God was showing mercy. This shadowed promise of a coming Savior is the first sign of hope that God will continue to build upon throughout the Bible. Genesis 3:15 is a promise that Jesus would come for his people, including you, me, and others all around the globe and across time.[2]

From this first act of rebellion, sin spread like a vicious, deadly disease, infecting the lives of everyone. By Genesis 6, sin has become so significant that God chooses to destroy the world through a flood, saving just Noah and his family. In doing so God is demonstrating that no matter how deep or pervasive our sin is, it is never strong enough to stop his plan of redemption.

By Genesis 11, after the flood, sin is just as significant as it had been before. In fact, in Genesis 11:1–9, people gather to build a tower to prove that they don't need God. In his judgment, God spread people across the globe and gave them different languages. By this judgment, people groups of different languages, cultures, and traditions dispersed throughout the world.

Promise

God's people were in deep need. Their sin had broken their relationship with God over and over again. Starting in Genesis 3:15 and moving onward, the Old Testament provides a progressively clearer picture of the Savior that God's people need, a picture that will be fully realized with the coming of Jesus Christ. As you take time to read over these passages of promise, remember that these are more than stories of the past. This is a promise for *you*: that one day God himself would take on flesh, move into your world, and save you from the effects of sin through his death and resurrection for you.

Genesis 12:1–3. God chose the nation of Israel to be both the recipient of God's love and the conduit of that same love to the nations around them. Although they were God's chosen people, his plan of redemption did not stop with them. From the very beginning of God's promise to Abraham, God said that the Savior of the world would come through Abraham and his people. All nations of the earth would be blessed through the promise of a Savior given to Israel.

The first Great Commission mandate of the Bible is found in Genesis 12:1–3. The people of Israel were God's witnesses to the world.[3] They were to be a witness of God's goodness and glory by welcoming other nations in and also by going out, as seen in the story of Jonah.[4] God called Israel into a deep relationship with himself, and through this intimate relationship, they were drawn out in love toward others. The people of Israel were blessed so that they could channel that blessing to the nations around them.

Exodus 9:13–16. As we read further in the story, we see that God's people were in slavery under the rule of a cruel Egyptian pharaoh. God sent Moses to deliver his people, but Pharaoh refused to listen. God sent plague after plague, but still Pharaoh refused to obey God, choosing instead his own glory and self-interests. God was clearly behind this story of judgment, making his name and power known to both Pharaoh and to the watching world. In verse 16, God tells Pharaoh, "But for this purpose I have raised you up, to show you my power, so that my name may be proclaimed in all the earth." God had a global purpose in the Exodus story. He was making his name known to the surrounding nations through the judgment of Pharaoh and the rescue of his people.

God was not just making himself know *through* Moses, he was also making himself known *to* Moses. As Moses was sent out on a mission to make God's glory known in Egypt, Moses was also drawn deeper into God's presence as he saw his weakness and desperate need for the Lord (Exodus 3:10–4:17; 33:12–23). As we look at the whole Exodus story, we see that God's just, powerful, and passionate pursuit of his chosen people revealed his character to the world.

Joshua 2:8–13. Here we see God's glory being revealed through the Exodus to a woman named Rahab. Rahab was a Gentile prostitute living in the infamous city of Jericho. Jericho was a walled city that stood as a gateway into the rest of Canaan, the land God had promised his people.[5] Spies were sent to Canaan to scout out the land. Because God had been working in Rahab's heart, she hid the spies from the king's men.

Before the Israelite spies arrived in the city, Rahab and the people of Jericho had already heard stories of the God of Israel displaying his power over the mighty Egyptian army. The people of Jericho were struck with fear. But Rahab's response to these stories was more significant. She both feared God and chose to follow him. The story of God's power drew her into the family of God.

Rahab became the first Canaanite convert and her life was spared in the fall of Jericho (Joshua 6). What is even more amazing is that God chose to use Rahab in his promise to send a Savior. Rahab would become the mother of Boaz, the husband of Ruth who was the great-grandmother of King David, a forerunner and ancestor of Jesus (Matthew 1:5–6). God often uses the least likely of people to join him in his story of redemption.

Psalm 67. The Psalms are a collection of songs that declare God's love and pursuit of his people. In fact, the Psalms contain more than 175 references to God's unfolding plan of redemption for all peoples.[6]

In Psalm 67, the psalmist writes of God being worthy of worship by all nations. He prays that God would bless Israel, and that through Israel he would bless the nations of the earth with the knowledge of himself. In fact, the text is clear in verses 1 and 2 that Israel has been chosen by God to be a blessing to the nations.

In a similar way today, God's people, the church, have also been blessed to be a blessing. We have received the good news of God's love for us through the cross. It has brought transformation and is giving us a new family. We can now channel that blessing to others.

Isaiah 49:1, 5–6. Isaiah prophesied of the coming servant, referring to Jesus. Through the prophet Isaiah, God was describing the promised Messiah as the one who will complete the mission of God to the ends of the earth. Jesus would not come just for the house of Israel but for every ethnic people group on earth, including you and me.

This messianic passage in Isaiah is important because it clearly communicates, along with many others, the global implications of God's plan of redemption. Israel was the start of a whole-world redemption that was God's plan all along. Jesus would gather the world back to God, to worship him and enjoy him forever.[7]

Jonah 4:11. The whole book of Jonah is a story of God's love and pursuit of the nations. God commissioned his prophet to go to the ungodly city of Nineveh to declare God's invitation to repentance, but Jonah refused to go. When he finally did go, he preached and the whole city turned to God. You would assume Jonah would praise God for his mercy, but instead he gets angry and says, "That is why I made haste to flee to Tarshish; for I knew that you are a gracious God and merciful, slow to anger and abounding in steadfast love, and relenting from disaster" (Jonah 4:2).

Jonah was infuriated by God's outrageous mercy to this Gentile city in allowing them to repent and turn to God. Jonah didn't see a foreign enemy like Nineveh as worthy of salvation, nor did he see how he was in need of God's outrageous mercy and grace himself. Jonah, God's messenger, was a sinner in need of God's mercy. God reminded Jonah of his need for him and, as we read in verse 11, God declared his great compassion and concern for the people of Nineveh, one of the great cities of the day. The book of Jonah shows us that God has love and concern for all peoples of the earth, both those who live in open rebellion against him, like the people of Nineveh, and even God's own servants, like his angry and reluctant missionary, Jonah.

God's pursuit of the nations in the Old Testament. We've looked at just a few of the many Scripture passages that unpack God's plan of redemption for all nations. Below is a fuller, yet still not comprehensive, list of passages that unpack the theme of missions in the Old Testament.

- Genesis 22:17–18
- Numbers 14:20–23
- Deuteronomy 10:17–19
- Joshua 4:23–24
- 2 Chronicles 6:32–33
- Psalm 2:7–12
- Psalm 22:26–28
- Psalm 108:3–6
- Isaiah 12
- Isaiah 52:6–10
- Micah 5:4
- Habakkuk 2:14
- Malachi 1:11

LESSON 2: GOD'S GLOBAL MISSION IN THE NEW TESTAMENT

PREPARATION AND INSTRUCTIONS

For the opening activity, have participants gather in groups to discuss the article, "Renewal Mission." The discussion question is in the student section of the book.

LEARNING OBJECTIVES

- To review how God's plan to redeem people from all nations has been in place from the beginning of time and is at the heart of who he is

- To see that the coming of Jesus is the fulfillment of a promise of love and redemption for all peoples on earth

LESSON CONTENT

Last week we opened our Bibles and walked through the Old Testament, seeing God's plan to bring his love and salvation to every nation on earth. We learned that missions is not just a New Testament idea. It flows throughout the whole Bible from Genesis to Revelation.

We looked at the concepts of creation, fall, and promise last week. Today, we will continue our journey through the Scriptures by seeing God's promise of a Savior fulfilled in the coming of Jesus. When Jesus came, he brought hope for the whole world. Let's open our Bibles and look further at God's glorious redemption plan for all peoples of the earth.

Take time to read each passage aloud as a large group or in smaller groups. You might encourage participants to mark the passages in their own Bibles and think through how they fit together to display the redeeming love of God.

Provision

Through God's grace and in fulfillment of his promises, he sent a Savior in Christ Jesus. Jesus, took on a human nature even to the point of being born as a helpless baby, so that he could save his people from their sins and bring them into life with God.

Luke 2:25–32. Shortly after Jesus was born, Mary and Joseph traveled to Jerusalem to take Jesus to the temple to be dedicated to the Lord. There they met a man named Simeon. The passage says Simeon was righteous and devout, and greatly longed for the coming of the Messiah. As Mary and Joseph brought Jesus into the temple, Simeon scooped the baby up into his arms and declared what the prophets had told all along: that this child was the Savior for all peoples, "a light for revelation to the Gentiles, and for glory to your people Israel." What the Old Testament only revealed as a shadow was now being brought to light.

As we have already seen and will continue to see throughout the narrative of Scripture, God's salvation plan is not only cosmic (impacting all people and places), it is also personal. The goodness and glory of God in human form touched the lives of real, everyday, salt-of-the-earth people.

Simeon was one of many who met Jesus, were changed by his presence, and experienced the promise of God fulfilled. The Savior had arrived.

John 3:16–17. This is a familiar passage, but before we quickly move past it, slow down and read it again. It gives us a foundation for God's global mission: his love. One of the foundational reasons for God's work of redemption is his love, both his character of love and the outworking of that love for us his people. Look again at verse 16, "For God so loved the world, that he gave his only Son." That statement should overwhelm us.

God's love compelled him to move out on mission to bring us back into a relationship with himself, a relationship rooted in love. This love is what should compel us out on mission as well. Even though we'll have many motivations for sharing Jesus and making disciples, let our primary motivation be love—God's love for us, and as a result, our love for others. God's love in us and working through us drives the mission of God forward.

This love that meets us, transforms us, and moves us out in obedience is more than simple duty—more than marching orders given to a soldier. A life of mission, empowered by the love of God, is a life of wonder and joy. As we walk with Jesus in his love and share that love with others, life itself become a delight, something we can truly enjoy.

John 4:1–45. Before we read the passage in our groups, let's take some time to understand the context of the story. Israel and the Samaritans had a long-standing feud going back hundreds of years. After a military defeat by the Assyrians, many of the Jews who remained in Samaria intermarried with foreigners and adhered to a false religion. Over the years, cultural tradition and practice for the Samaritans evolved, and Jews outside of Samaria saw the Samarians as "half-breed" Jews who had abandoned right worship. By the first century, the Samarians had developed their own form of Judaism, no longer looked to Jerusalem as their holy city, and had a mutual hatred for the Israelites.[8]

Samaritans had long resisted the right worship of God (Ezra 4). This means they were one of the lost nations Simeon had spoken of in Luke 2:30–32, "For my eyes have seen your salvation that you have prepared in the presence of all peoples, a light for revelation to the Gentiles, and for glory to your people Israel."

GROUP DISCUSSION. If your group is large, have participants break up into cohorts to read the passage aloud and discuss the following questions:

- *As you read this story, what stands out to you about how Jesus engaged with the Samaritan woman and led her to understand the gospel?*

- *How did the gospel impact this woman and her community and why is this story so important for understanding God's love for the nations?*

It's significant to note that Jesus, a Jewish man, breaks all kinds of cultural norms to simply talk with a Samaritan woman. Often, Jewish men did not talk to women in public, and Israelites definitely did not associate with Samaritans. But the gospel changes things. It brings hope and life across ethnic and cultural barriers. Where walls once existed, bridges are built. Jesus's whole life was marked by engaging those at the margins along with the cultural elite. He walked with common men every day for three years, ate with notorious sinners, and, as we see here, brought the gospel to a foreign woman and used her to carry the gospel to a whole village. By Jesus traveling through Samaria, stopping at the well, and intentionally talking with the woman at the well, Jesus was bringing the gospel to the nations.

Multiplication

God not only came to call a people to himself, but also to give his people a mission. That mission is the same redemption mission God has been accomplishing throughout history. Now through his people, the church, God is calling us to live on mission by sharing Jesus with others, making and multiplying disciples, and planting new churches.

Matthew 28:18–20. This familiar passage is one of five Great Commission passages found in the New Testament that articulate a call and vision for God's people to be moving forward with the gospel (Mark 16:15–6; Luke 24:46–48; John 20:21–23; Acts 1:8). Matthew 28:18–20 is significant because if provides a fuller picture of this mission. Look at the passage again. What elements of mission do we see clearly?

- Jesus's authority over all things
- A call to make disciples
- Making disciples of all nations
- Baptizing them in God's triune name
- Teaching new Christians God's Word
- Remembering that Jesus is present with us

As you can see, these words from Jesus—some of his last before his ascension—lay a foundation for the church and for all of us in how we should be both giving the gospel out (evangelism and disciple-making) and taking the gospel in (becoming disciples, sitting under the teaching of God's Word). What is just as amazing is that Jesus promises us that as we go out, he will always be with us.

2 Timothy 2:1–2. As we move out toward others with the gospel, in both declaration and demonstration, God compels us to not only share but also to make disciples—to help people grow as committed followers of Jesus. Here Paul writes to his son in the faith, Timothy, and urges him to invest in (disciple) people who will also invest in others. The call here for us is to help make disciples who, in turn, also make other disciples.

It is amazing to consider that part of God's great plan of redemption includes using you and me to invest our lives in others who will then turn around and do the same. Not perfect discipleship, but faithful discipleship. When we invest our lives in others, in both big and small ways, we are seeing God's plan for the nations unfold.

Romans 15:20–21. The gospel spread like wildfire when the Holy Spirit fell on the disciples and empowered the church to live on mission (Acts 2). Persecution and oppression came hard against the church, but through people like Paul and others, the gospel continued to spread. Just as we saw throughout the Old Testament, God continues to use broken people living in a broken world to bring about his global mission.

In Romans 15, Paul writes to the Christians in Rome and tells them that the ministry God had given him from Jerusalem to Illyricum was completed. His desire now is to go where the gospel is not. Paul's calling is to share the gospel, make disciples, and start new churches to the ends of the earth. Paul models the movement the church is called to embrace in global mission: growing in love for God as we take the gospel to people who have little to no access.

From the early church, to the ministry of Paul, and onward for the last two thousand years, God has been making his name known through his people, the church. As we are renewed through missions, God's kingdom grows in our hearts and we go out in love to others.

Fulfillment

God began a plan of redemption back in Genesis that he carries out through the whole Bible. God's redemption mission is to save people to himself, people from all nations and people groups on the earth.

Revelation 7:9–12. The New Testament documents the spread of the gospel throughout the known world. Fast-forward two thousand years to today, and the task of missions is still before us. How can we ever hope to take the message of salvation to all peoples on earth? At times, this task can seem impossible. But Revelation 7 is a promise that God will fulfill his mission—and God always keeps his promises.

That's why Revelation 7 is such an encouragement. It paints a picture of God finishing what he started. Believers from every nation, tribe, people, and language will stand before God for all of eternity and worship him in all his glory. When we think about the massive task given to the church, we see that it's not that missions *must* be finished—it's that missions *will* be finished.

Reaching people with the gospel, multiplying disciples, and planting new churches around the globe is a daunting task. It's a task we could never do in our own strength. The beauty of missions is that God is the one working out this redemption story in the world and in our own lives as well. And through his kindness, you and I get to play a role in making his name known to others.

Take heart, God will finish what he started. Revelation 7 is a reminder that God keeps his promises.

LESSON 3: NECESSITY OF MISSIONS
PREPARATION AND INSTRUCTIONS

For the opening activities, have participants gather in groups to discuss the article, "God's Wrath Against Sin."

Read and discuss Matthew 25:31–46, and then have groups pray together.

LEARNING OBJECTIVES

- To understand the concept of God's wrath against sin and the reality of hell

- To understand that Jesus, through his death and resurrection, is the path to life with God both here on earth and for all eternity

- In community with others, to wrestle with the exclusivity of Jesus and what happens to those who never hear the gospel

LESSON CONTENT

It's not hard to get excited about global missions. We hear stories, read powerful statistics, travel to places without a strong gospel presence, and come away firmly believing that doing missions is an urgent need. But before we quit our jobs and move overseas, we need to stop and ask ourselves: Is missions really necessary? Is reaching people with the gospel, making disciples, and planting new churches an essential endeavor?

Let's be clear from the beginning: missions *is* necessary. But before we move on, we need to take time to answer three core theological questions addressing the necessity of missions.

1. What is the wrath of God that leads to eternal separation from him?

2. Is Jesus the only way to eternal life?

3. What happens to those who never hear the gospel of Jesus?

In the article you read before today's class, we walked through the reality of God's wrath against sin and the truth that hell is a real place of punishment for those who do not follow Jesus. As hard as this truth is, understanding God's wrath is vital. Without the truth that God is holy and will fully judge sin, there would be no reason for Jesus to come to earth and give his life for broken sinners like you and me. There would be no need for mission work. But God's wrath against sin is real, which makes the life, death, and resurrection of Jesus necessary if we and all nations are to experience eternal life with God.

Is Jesus the Only Way to Eternal Life?

In light of this reality, the question is often raised, "Is Jesus the only way to eternal life or are their other paths to God?" This is a difficult question to wrestle with in the Western world and many other places around the globe, where the culture leans toward openness and tolerance at the expense of absolute truth, especially the truth about what happens after a person dies. No matter what country or context you find yourself in, if you are actively sharing your Christian faith you will often be met with resistance. You might be labeled intolerant or closed-minded. You might even suffer persecution for sharing the gospel with others.

Hostility toward the exclusive claims of Christianity is not a new phenomenon. Since the early days of the church, the exclusiveness of faith in Jesus was met with resistance and was labeled offensive, even as the gospel spread around the world.

Jesus, One Among Many?

NOTE: Teachers, you can read this first-person story from the author to the class or ask them to turn to the story in their own copy of the Leader's Guide and take turns reading it aloud together.

> As a young man I (Nathan) served in the country of Nepal as mid-term missionary. I had joined a ministry team of others, both Western and Nepali, who were focused on doing evangelism and strengthening churches in remote

villages. Early on in my ministry I developed a friendship Hari, a young Nepali leader, and we had begun traveling together to do ministry.

On one trip out to a village, we were met with open arms. Although this village was almost completely Hindu, many in the village were open to hearing more about the person of Jesus. While Hari shared the gospel in the local school, I sat with two of the village elders and told them the story of the gospel from creation to the resurrection of Jesus. When we got to the point in the story where Jesus began his ministry, these village elders were enthralled with who Jesus was and what he did on earth. They even stopped me several times in the story to ask questions about Jesus.

After the story was over, I asked my new friends what they thought—what the story meant to them. They spoke deeply kind words about Jesus, the story of the Bible, and the Christian faith. But when I kindly, yet firmly, pressed in about Jesus's exclusive claims to be Savior and their need to trust in Jesus, the elders' demeanor changed. It was clear that they were offended. Through a harsh tone, they told me they were happy to add Jesus to their collection of gods, but to say that Jesus must be followed exclusively was foolish.

This experience taught me that many people are open to the person of Jesus. Some even embrace his claims to be God. But to say he is the only way and that other ways are false turns people against the gospel. These village elders were willing to add Jesus and even his divinity to their other countless gods of Hinduism, but they would not reject their idols and follow Jesus exclusively.

Sadly, the world around us often relates to Jesus the same way these elders did. Whether it be Hinduism, Buddhism, cultural Christianity, or popular culture, a growing number of people reject the exclusive claims of Jesus.

As we think about the question of whether Jesus is the only way to eternal life, it's helpful to understand the key terms of *pluralism, inclusivism,* and *exclusivism.* Although this classic theological paradigm has its limits, it provides a general framework for the exclusiveness of Christ.[9]

Pluralism is the belief that all paths lead to God, and Jesus is not unique. Nathan's experience in Nepal shows the view that the path to God is all-inclusive. The village elders appreciated Jesus, even had a fondness for him. However, they clearly thought Christianity was Nathan's path to eternal life, and they had their own. This is a pluralism lived out. Timothy Tennent writes that pluralists "believe that the world's religions provide independent access to salvation. . . . Christianity is just one among many religions and has no unique claim as the final or authoritative truth."[10]

Pluralism says that absolute truth must be fluid and the path to truth, existence, and the afterlife is determined by a person's own belief structure, not by a rigid religious structure imposed from the outside. In the framework of pluralism, saying there is only one way to God and eternal life is arrogant, even hateful.

Inclusivism is the belief that Christianity and the work of Jesus are uniquely true, but it is possible to be saved apart from faith in Christ in this lifetime.[11] By this view, Jesus is necessary for salvation, but our individual response of repentance and faith in him is not necessary. Sadly, this is a growing view of some in the church today, especially in the Western world. Much of this pull toward inclusivism comes from a lack of personal biblical literacy, a response to emotion (it feels better), personal experience ("I know a good person who died without Jesus"), and pressure from a pluralistic culture ("I don't want to be seen as intolerant").

As popular culture presses the idea that all paths lead to God, Christians who are not grounded in God's Word can struggle to reconcile what their faith tells them with what the world around them says. One response to this pressure is to take a more middle-ground approach that says Jesus is unique and necessary but that those who are good, devout people will also be given eternal life (inclusivism). As nice as this sounds, the view of inclusivism simply does not fit the Bible's teaching.

Exclusivism is the belief that the only way to God and to eternal life is through the life, death, and resurrection of Jesus. This eternal life is only given through faith in the work of Christ. Therefore, to be saved from eternal judgment, one must hear and believe the gospel of Jesus in this life.[12]

If we take the Bible seriously about its own claims, we come to the conclusion that there is no way to God or eternal life apart from Jesus. The New Testament is covered with exclusive claims to the saving nature of Jesus's work on the cross.

- **John 3:16** is the most famous passage on God's pursuing love for the world, yet often we fail to read this passage within its context. God's great love for the world is a love that demands a response. "For God so loved the world, that he gave his only Son, that whoever believes in him should not perish but have eternal life. For God did not send his Son into the world to condemn the world, but in order that the world might be saved through him. Whoever believes in him is not condemned, but whoever does not believe is condemned already.... Whoever believes in the Son has eternal life; whoever does not obey the Son shall not see life, but the wrath of God remains on him" (John 3:16–18, 36). This passage teaches that Jesus came not to condemn the world but to save it. However, those who do not follow Jesus as Savior stand condemned and sit under God's wrath.

- Jesus speaks about his own exclusive work of salvation again in **John 14:6.** "I am the way, and the truth, and the life. No one comes to the Father except through me." Jesus makes the path to salvation as clear as possible. He alone provides a way back into a restored relationship with God and the hope of eternal life.

- Peter makes a similar claim to the exclusiveness of salvation through Jesus in **Acts 4**. In this passage, Peter and John were preaching to a crowd in Jerusalem when the Sadducees and the temple guard arrested and questioned them. Peter and John boldly proclaimed the exclusiveness of Christ. Peter was "filled with the Holy Spirit" (v. 8) and preached a powerful evangelistic sermon to those who murdered Jesus. He boldly proclaims in verse 12, "And there is salvation in no one else, for there is no other name under heaven given among men by which we must be saved." This story puts the power and reach of the gospel on full display. God's pursuing love extends even to the very men who crucified Jesus. The gospel knows no bounds!

If there were any other way to God, any other way to be rescued from sin and death, why did Jesus come and give his life for us? It is clear from Scripture that Jesus came to save a people in need of rescue. Jesus entered into our world, clothed in flesh, living in full humanity, showing compassion and hope to us, **and ultimately dying on the cross and being raised again**, because we need a restored relationship with God. However, don't be mistaken and think God's hand was somehow forced. The triune God—Father, Son, and Holy Spirit—planned from before the creation of the world to send Jesus to bring us back into life with him (Ephesians 1:4–10). Yes, the incarnation, Jesus's brutal death, and his resurrection are God's great plan of redemption for all nations—and specifically, his great rescue plan for you. Because of the gospel, you can now experience life with God both now and in the world to come.

As we sit under this teaching about God's wrath and the exclusive claims of Jesus, it can be easy to feel the hardness of these doctrines with our realizing the joy found in them. God did not leave us in our sin and suffering. Jesus is the exclusive path to a right relationship with God, to life with him in the here and now, and to eternal life with him. The fact that Jesus made a way for us should bring us hope and drive us to a life of gratitude lived out in joyful worship.

What Happens to Those Who Never Hear the Gospel?

This raises the question: If Jesus is the only way to a restored relationship with God and to eternal life, what happens to those who never hear the gospel? What happens to those who remain in their sin?

GROUP DISCUSSION: In your groups, read through these two passages: Romans 1:18–25 and John 3:16–19, then discuss the following questions:

- *What details from these passages stand out to you?*

- *What are the biblical authors seeking to communicate in each passage?*

Key Truth: Each of the passages you just read addresses the exclusive claims of Christ, including what happens to a person who does not turn from sin and follow Jesus in this life. The Bible is clear: there is only one way to God and eternal life, and that way is through faith in Jesus who died and rose again. It is important to remember that there are no innocent people. "The fool says in his heart, 'There is no God.' They are corrupt, they do abominable deeds, there is none who does good. The LORD looks down from heaven on the children of man, to see if there are any who understand, who seek after God. They have all turned aside; together they have become corrupt; there is none who does good, not even one" (Psalm 14:1–3).

All people are guilty of rebelling against God. We all have chosen sin, but by God's grace through his Son, he has provided a way back to himself.

God's call to share Jesus and make disciples was more than just a nice idea—more than a suggestion. The church is called to take the gospel across the street and across the world because people need to hear who Jesus is and what he has done for them. Without the gospel, there is no hope. But the gospel brings hope wherever it goes. The gospel provides a path to life—life with Jesus today and for all eternity.

Conclusion

This whole lesson points us to the fact that missions—reaching people with the gospel, making disciples, and planting churches—is necessary.

Not only is it necessary, but it is a picture of God's love for us. Because sin leads to eternal death and God's wrath against sin is real, Jesus provided a way to life through his own death and resurrection. The call to missions makes no sense unless God's wrath against sin is real and Jesus is the only way to eternal life. These truths should motivate us to the necessity and urgency of the missionary task. We take the gospel to the lost through the power of the Holy Spirit because without the gospel, people are eternally lost and separated from God.

As you reflect on these hard truths this week, also consider how these truths can move you closer to God and deeper into God's global missions. How does God want to use you to make his love known?

LESSON 4: HISTORY OF MISSIONS
PREPARATION AND INSTRUCTIONS

This lesson will look at the history of missions—how God has been on the move through men, women, and churches throughout history. Although our primary focus will be on cross-cultural missions, we also know that God moves through ordinary people wherever they find themselves. Have someone from your local church who is actively sharing their faith in their everyday life come and share their story of how they are living on mission and making disciples where God has placed them.

- Ask them to share their testimony of living on mission, including a story of success and one of struggle.
- Ask about their common mission practices.
- Ask what encouragement would they give to those seeking to live as someone who is sent.

For the lesson, you might want to find pictures of the missionaries and mission groups mentioned and include those in your lesson presentation.

LEARNING OBJECTIVES
- To help participants see how God has been at work in every generation to expand his kingdom

- To provide a broad survey of the modern Protestant missions movement that came from the Western world
- To highlight key figures in missions history, giving depth and personality to the history of missions

LESSON CONTENT

On the outside, cross-cultural ministry and the life of a missionary can seem like a grand adventure with Jesus: missionaries work among the lost in remote places and experience the Christian life like few others do. But although there is truth in this thinking, a closer look shows that life on the mission field entails much more, including loneliness, culture shock, conflict, suffering, and the grueling nature of language learning and cross-cultural ministry. When we take a look behind the curtain of cross-cultural missions, we can see a clearer picture of how God has worked through his church—around the world and across time—as we study missions history.

Missions history reminds us of God's goodness in the past, and gives us courage to press on to the promises of tomorrow. History is full of the stories of God using broken vessels, people like you and me, to make his name known to people shrouded in spiritual darkness.

What we know as modern-day missions started in the middle of the 1700s. Before then, missions was primarily a Roman Catholic endeavor, although not exclusively.[13] There were some small ventures into global missions including John Calvin's church planting in France and sending missionaries to Brazil, but these were simply shadows of what was coming.

God was doing several different things to bring global missions back to the forefront of his church, including the Great Awakenings in England and America, the printing press, and the stirring of a small group of Christians in Eastern Europe.

Ludwig Von Zinzendorf and the Moravians[14]

Ludwig Von Zinzendorf was born in 1700 into a wealthy family in lower Austria. Through the Reformation, his family became Lutherans. He was educated by his Christian grandmother and this had a lasting impact on his life. He trained to be a lawyer but decided to settle down and become a landowner instead, buying what would later be known as Herrnhut.

Zinzendorf received Christian refugees on his land who had fled religious persecution from a nearby area (modern-day Czech Republic). This group would come to be known as the Moravians.

After Zinzendorf met a former slave from the West Indies and a native from Greenland who had both been converted to Christianity, he was impassioned for missions and took this passion back to the Moravians. By the time of Zinzendorf's death, the Moravians had sent out 226 missionaries in teams to at least thirteen locations.[15] This sending movement became one of the first in Protestant history. In fact, in the short period of this missions movement, the Moravians sent out more people to the nations than the Protestant church had in the previous two hundred years.[16]

God used Zinzendorf and the Moravians to start a missions movement that continues to influence Protestant missions to this very day. They serve as a reminder that innovation in the service of the gospel is one essential way God grows his kingdom. Even today we draw on the Moravians for ideas like missions agencies, business as mission, and the modern version of a team-based approach to missions.

Their history is also marked with great sacrifice including some Moravians selling themselves into slavery to better reach slaves for Christ. William Danker writes, "The most important contribution of the Moravians was their emphasis that every Christian is a missionary and should witness through his daily vocation."[17] Zinzendorf and the members of the early Moravian church launched a worldwide missionary movement that prepared the way for William Carey and the modern missions movement that would follow.[18]

Coastland Missions (1700–1910): William Carey, George Liele

At this point, global missions was still considered a strange concept in the Protestant church. William Carey felt this problem deeply, and became one of the main figures God used to help awaken the Western church to global missions. The first wave was focused on the coastal areas of the world.

Carey was a cobbler and lay preacher in England. He had a growing conviction that God had called Christians to take the gospel to the nations, but others were either indifferent to the idea or outright opposed. One day, Carey gathered with other Baptist leaders and shared his biblical vision for missions. One leader stood up and said, "Young man, sit down. When God pleases to convert the heathen, he will do it without your aid or mine."[19] Carey, however, would not back down. In 1792, he published a small booklet that would help usher in the modern missions movement and the first Protestant missions agency.[20]

Carey would go on to be the first missionary sent from this new missions agency. He spent a lifetime in India, pouring his life out for the gospel. He is known for being a church planter, linguist, botanist, and Bible translator—contributing to Bible translation in thirty-six different languages.[21] Carey is known as the "Father of Modern Missions" for his overall contribution in helping the movement get started and because of the impact he made in missions theory and practice.

There are so many other significant figures that could be discussed in this era of missions, but George Liele is one that stands out. Liele was an African American missionary who has much to teach us about perseverance, determination, and building the kingdom of God.

Some of the earliest known missionaries sent from America were David George, Moses Baker, Prince Williams, and George Liele. They were all African Americans who were slaves before the United States became a nation. Liele is considered America's first missionary. He chose to leave America in 1782 to start a church in Kingston, Jamaica. This was ten years before William Carey left England for India, and twenty years before Adoniram Judson left America for Burma.

Liele was born a slave in Virginia and was later given his freedom so that he could pursue his call to ministry.[22] He was ordained in a white church in Georgia and started the first African American church in America.

God used Liele mightily to plant new churches and lead others to faith in the US, but Liele feared being re-enslaved by the heirs of his former enslaver, so he sold himself to be an indentured servant in Jamaica.[23] Both during and after working off his debt in Jamaica, God continued to use Liele to impact people with the gospel.

Liele never received pay for his pastoral ministry or missionary work, yet he became the first Protestant missionary to go out from America to establish a foreign mission. As a preacher and missionary, Liele shared the gospel with thousands, baptizing hundreds of new Christians. In 1819, there were eight thousand Baptists in Jamaica, but by 1832 there were more than twenty thousand.[24] George Lisle had a significant role in this growth.

Not only was George Liele an effective pastor and missionary, he was a mobilizer for global missions. Through his discipleship and influence, new works were started in Georgia, Nova Scotia, and Sierra Leone.[25] Both William Carey and George Liele remind us of the need to continue to do pioneering missions work which sets aside comfort and ease in order to bring the gospel to those who have not yet heard about Christ.

Inland Missions (1865–1980): Hudson Taylor, Amy Carmichael

Until this point, most global missions focused on engaging peoples and cultures near the coastlands, which boat travel made easily accessible. One man who led the move from the coastlands to the interior was Hudson Taylor. Taylor served as a missionary from England to China in the mid- to late-1800s. His desire to reach the interior of China opened the door for missions around the world to move away from the coast and deep into harder-to-reach areas.

Taylor is known for pushing back against the European mission establishment, taking on Chinese dress and customs, and mobilizing thousands of new missionaries for China, many of them students. Ruth Tucker writes, "Few missionaries in the nineteen centuries since the apostle Paul have had a wider vision and have carried out a more systematic plan of evangelizing a broad geographic area than did James Hudson Taylor."[26]

Amy Carmichael is another example of the many faithful missionaries who labored long and hard to see the gospel take root in unreached places. At the end of the nineteenth century, Carmichael, a single woman, left her life of wealth in Ireland to serve first in Japan and then in India. Carmichael poured her life out for more than fifty years among the most marginalized people in India. She was a model of sacrifice and love, for both those she worked among and the watching world.

Carmichael established the Dohnavur Fellowship, a small group of people committed to serving orphans who had experienced sexual abuse at Hindu temples. She was known to be a bit eccentric and to drive her coworkers harder than needed.[27] Yet, despite these significant shortcomings, God used her and the ministry she established to make a lasting impact in India and beyond. She wrote numerous books and inspired a generation of future missionaries. She is one example of the many single women throughout missions history who have given their lives to global missions. Some include Lottie Moon, Gladys Aylward, Betsey Stockton, and Lilias Trotter, among others. Taken as a whole, the era of inland missions illustrates the importance of setting aside our own cultural norms in order to live among, love, and serve those we are trying to reach with the message of the gospel.

People Groups (1935–present): Jim and Elisabeth Elliot, Back to Jerusalem

As missionaries and mission societies continued to press into the interior of Asia, Africa, and South America, a new movement in missions began. There came a growing awareness that missions was more than just reaching a political nation with the gospel. One of several key events that sparked this new era happened at the Lausanne Conference, a global gathering of Christian leaders in 1974. Ralph Winter stood up to speak and challenged the traditional understanding of missions. Winter made it clear that the driving goal of missions was not to reach every geopolitical nation (the common view of the day) but to reach every ethnic people group. He and others helped leaders in the Christian world understand that the "nations" written about in the Bible (*ethnos* in Matthew 28:19) referred to the thousands of different ethnic and linguistic groups that make up our world.

There are numerous missionaries we could study in the era of people groups, but let's look at the lives of Jim and Elisabeth Elliot. Though their story is tragic, God used it to help inspire several generations of future missionaries.

Both Jim and Elisabeth had moved separately to Ecuador to be cross-cultural missionaries, focused on people groups in the jungle of Ecuador. While there, they married and started a family. During this time, Jim and four of his friends became passionate about the Waorani people and began engaging them.

The Waorani tribe had little to no access to the outside world, so these five men began taking trips to fly over the jungle region to drop gifts and make contact. On one occasion, they landed on a sandy beach to make face-to-face contact and all five men were murdered by members of the tribe.

What's even more startling than the sacrificial death of these five men is the fact that Elisabeth Elliot and Rachel Saint, the sister of one of the fallen missionaries, continued to engage the Waorani people. Many of those in the tribe placed their faith in Jesus and churches were planted. To this day there continues to be a vibrant Waorani church. Elisabeth wrote several books telling their missionary story including *Through the Gates of Splendor*.

Much of written mission history focuses on engagement from the West to the rest of the world, but there are vast numbers of other untold stories of believers around the world who've taken the gospel across language and cultures, often at significant sacrifice. The Back to Jerusalem movement is one of those stories.

In the 1920s, a group of Chinese church leaders caught a vision for taking the gospel to peoples and places between China and Jerusalem along the Silk Road. Their desire was to see the gospel make a full circle back to where it began, in Jerusalem. The early days of this Chinese missions movement saw great persecution, and it was forced underground. But it didn't die.

The movement was reignited when Simon Zhao, an early leader, was released from prison in 1984. Zhao had been sentenced to forty years, but each day he set his face toward Jerusalem and all the people groups in between, and he prayed, "God, the vision that you've given us has perished, but I pray you'll raise up a new generation of Chinese believers to fulfill this vision."[28] God used him, and others, to send thousands of missionaries all over Asia, the Middle East, and beyond. The vision of the Back to Jerusalem movement is to send 100,000 missionaries to fifty-one countries around the world. The movement continues to this day.

Future of Missions (2000–future)

We are currently living in two missions eras, the people-group era and the future-of-missions era. We don't know exactly what this era will be known for or how it will play out, but it's clear that new and exciting things are happening. Moving into a new missions era teaches us one important principle in global missions: missions is dynamic, not static. Missions does not stay the same but changes as the world around us changes. The gospel never changes, but the way we reach people with the gospel must adjust and develop constantly. We are reminded that God continues to be faithful to raise up new movements and people to accomplish his purposes in the world. The following are a few of the major concepts that are shaping the future of missions:

- **Global South missions.** The center of missions sending has shifted to the Global South—the regions of Asia, Africa, and Latin America.[29] Countries that were once primarily receiving missionaries are now sending them in large numbers, so that what was once "the West to the rest" is now "from everywhere to everywhere." Countries like South Korea, Brazil, China, the Philippines, and others have become powerful sending forces. For example, in 2015 there were 35,000 international missions from Brazil and 30,000 missionaries sent out from churches in South Korea.[30] This shift in missions sending should be both a wakeup call to Western churches to continue to send, and a reason to celebrate. Praise God for using his global church to reach his global people.

- **Technology.** The internet, expanded cell service, transportation advancements, social media, and other technological advancements are changing the way we do cross-cultural ministry. These are advancements to be celebrated, learned from, and harnessed for gospel impact.

- **Urbanization and globalization.** Our world is rapidly becoming an urban place. More than 50 percent of the global population now lives in cities and that number is only increasing. This means that people groups who were once isolated are now living in large cities with hundreds of other people groups. The way we do missions must adapt to this growing urban reality.

The history of missions is vital to understand, learn from, and be motivated by. Not only is the past important, but so is the future. The future of missions has yet to be written, but it will be shaped by ordinary people like you and me who are used by an extraordinary God. As we think about God's faithfulness in missions history, let's look at several lessons to consider.

First, missions history is not something we should rush past because it illustrates God's faithfulness and power to accomplish his desires. The gift of history is that it teaches us lessons we take with us into the future. It allows us to look back at people, places, and events to see how they all fit together. We see stories of courage and justice alongside stories of evil and despair. When we slow down and study the history of the church, we learn how God worked in the past, and this gives us hope that he will continue to work in our future.

Second, God often uses the least likely of people to accomplish the most amazing things. The men and women that God has used to grow his kingdom—missionaries like Carey, Judson, Carmichael, and Elliot—struggled with sin, weakness, and doubts. They were men and women like you and me, wrestling with the brokenness of their own hearts and fighting to trust the Lord. One common thread in all of these stories is that they offered their lives up to God, rooted their lives in him, and depended on him in the very real struggles of life.

Finally, God has always been at work both in and through his people, even when we could not see it. God is a God on the move. Even when his plan of redemption seems slow, or absent at times, God is at work behind the scenes. Just because we don't have a written record of God working in a specific people or period of time does not mean he was not there. Heaven will be filled with surprising stories of God's mercy poured out in ages and in places where our history books remain silent.

God will continue to work through his church to bring about his goodness and glory in the world. And he will do his work through ordinary people. People like you and me. People who love him and give what gifts they have to serve the kingdom of God.

How has God gifted and empowered you to make his name known in this world?

LESSON 5: CHURCH ON MISSION
PREPARATION AND INSTRUCTIONS

For the opening questions about the mission of the church, you might want to provide groups/cohorts with markers and large tear-off sheets of paper, or arrange the sheets on walls around the room. Instruct participants to record their answers on the large sheets of paper. Make sure you have energy and excitement for the topic. You might share a personal story to get further engagement. Questions like these can often produce shallow answers, so push groups to dig deep, think creatively, and root their answers in Scripture.

As you teach the lesson, remember that it includes four key calls God has given the church to be about. In your teaching, make sure you connect all four calls. Remind participants that all their missions activity should be rooted in their life with God.

The goal of this lesson is not to spark debates about what we think the church's mission should be, but to provide a biblical overview of the mission God has given the church. It's a big topic, and as the leader, you can add detail and nuance as you see fit.

LEARNING OBJECTIVES

- To understand that God has called his church, and therefore every Christian, to be active in four key activities: (1) abiding with him and worshipping him, (2) sharing the gospel, (3) making and multiplying disciples, and (4) starting new and healthy churches

- To help participants begin to discover where their lives intersect with these truths

LESSON CONTENT

God gave Jesus a *message* and a *mission* on earth. The message and mission God gave his Son has been given to us, the church, as well. We, the church, are called to bring the good news of Jesus to a broken and dying world.

Our *message* is the gospel. Jesus, the promised one, came to earth to fulfill the mission God gave him. He lived a perfect life, testified of God's kingdom, died, and was raised to life to satisfy God's wrath and provide a way to eternal life.

The *mission* God the Father gave his Son was to save us from death and secure our adoption into the family of God. The question to wrestle with today is: *What is the mission God has given the church?* Although there is significant depth to the Bible's answer, for our purposes we will look at the mission of the church as four key calls God has given us to live out:

1. Abide with God and worship him.

2. Share Jesus with others.

3. Make and multiply disciples.

4. Start healthy churches.

Keep in mind, when we talk about God calling his church to live as sent people—people on mission with him—it means these four calls are for *you* as well!

Abide with God and Worship Him

The article you read already addressed the core call God has placed on our lives: the call to root our lives in Christ and abide with him. An indispensable aspect of abiding is to be rooted in a local church, worshipping and growing in community with others. The abiding life with Jesus is not solitary affair. We cannot experience the Christian life in all its depth and beauty unless we experience it in community with others. This is most fully realized when we are committed to and a part of a healthy local church.

Corporate worship, sitting under the teaching of God's Word, confessing our sins to one another, living lives of hospitality, and other aspects of doing life in a local church are vital to an abiding life with God. God's call to his church is a call to worship. It's a call to himself—a call to life in him, walking with others in community, embracing a life of worship, seeking to be transformed, while enjoying life in God's kingdom here on earth.

Along with a life of worship through abiding, God calls his people to be on a mission to the world.

Share Jesus with Others

Our life *with* God leads us into ministry *for* God. Our life *with* God is not just a "me-and-Jesus" life, it is a life lived in community with others. So it makes sense that the second key call we'll discuss is the call to share Jesus and his gospel with others. "And he said to them, 'Go into all the world and proclaim the gospel to the whole creation. Whoever believes and is baptized will be saved, but whoever does not believe will be condemned'" (Mark 16:15–16).

After the resurrection of Jesus, before he ascended to heaven, he gave his disciples the task of making the gospel known to the whole world. This is an enormous task but Jesus promised to give them the Holy Spirit to empower and lead them. As crazy as it sounds, Jesus's plan was to use his ragtag group of disciples to spread the gospel to the ends of the earth. That's still Jesus's plan today—to use his disciples, the church, to make his name and glory known to the nations of the earth.

Paul teaches this same truth in 2 Corinthians 5:20. He reminds us that God is making the gospel known to a watching world through us. "Therefore, we are ambassadors for Christ, God making his appeal through us. We implore you on behalf of Christ, be reconciled to God."

God's commission to us to make his name known has implications near and far. The call to make Jesus known is not only a call to global missions, but also a call to share Jesus with those around you in the everyday parts of your life. This includes both what we say and what we do. Jesus and his disciples were constantly meeting people's physical needs as they shared the life-giving message of the gospel. Sharing Jesus with others integrates our words and our deeds in ways that help others see Jesus more clearly and experience his transforming message more directly.

As I've talked with missions pastors over the years, they often tell me stories of pastoring people who love global missions and desire to make Jesus known but fail to live out that same passion in their everyday lives. Missions (evangelism, discipleship, and church planting) became a future possibility rooted in a far-off place instead of a current reality in their present lives.

The gospel is meant for both where we are and where we're not. God's desire for us as the church is to make Jesus known through the everyday rhythms of our lives *and* outward to places that have little to no access to the gospel. It's a both/and, not an either/or. God desires the gospel to go to the ends of the earth, starting in our own hearts and then in the lives of people we encounter every day. Our prayer should be, "Let the gospel go forth into the darkest places on earth, starting in my own heart and my own community!" May we be people who make Jesus known wherever we plant out feet, both across the street *and* across the globe.

Ask yourself, are you sharing the gospel in the place where God has you now? If not, why not? God desires for all of us to live our lives on mission, sharing the gospel with our words and demonstrating the gospel through our deeds wherever we find ourselves. At the same time, he also wants us to be active in making the gospel known among the unreached and forgotten peoples around the world. Think of it this way: the calling to bring the gospel to those in your everyday life doesn't change when you go overseas. The neighborhood may change, but the calling to share the gospel with your neighbor doesn't. *Sharing the gospel is less about location and more about obedience.*

GROUP DISCUSSION: Instruct participants to take a moment in their groups and think about whom God has placed in their lives right now that needs to hear the gospel. Ask participants to:

- *Write down one or two people who come to mind.*

- *Write down one practical step they can take toward sharing the gospel with those people.*

As you think about evangelism in your own life, fight the urge to get discouraged or to bury yourself under a mountain of shame. Yes, there are some in the church that are more gifted in evangelism. The Holy Spirit has gifted them to share Jesus more naturally and that is a beautiful thing. However, God's call for his people does not change. Even if you are gifted in others ways, the invitation to you is to step out of what is comfortable and declare the message of the gospel. As we will see in later lessons, there are many ways to share the gospel in which your gifts and passions intersect with opportunities to declare Jesus to others.

Make and Multiply Disciples

A disciple is simply a follower or learner of a master. When we talk about being a Christian disciple, we are talking about being followers and learners of the Master, Jesus Christ.

Discipleship is not just for new believers. Discipleship is the journey all believers take as they learn from and grow to become more like Christ. Discipleship is interwoven with the call to abide in God because it is our ever-deepening relationship with God that drives discipleship. It is important to remember that even as we make disciples, we have not arrived ourselves. We are still and will continue to be disciples until we see Jesus face-to-face. Discipleship is both something we are experiencing and something we help others experience.

Zane Pratt writes about four traits of a disciple, traits that provide a helpful gauge to measure our own discipleship journey and help others grow as disciples.[31] A disciple is someone who:

1. Walks intimately with Jesus
2. Not only soaks in the teaching of Jesus but adopts his character and way of life
3. Becomes so much like their master Jesus that they remind others of him
4. Makes new disciples

GROUP DISCUSSION: Have participants refer to the four traits in their books. Ask them to discuss the following questions:

- *Which of these discipleship traits is most challenging for you?*

- *How do you think God is calling you to grow in this area?*

The concept of discipleship is rooted in the Great Commission. In the passage in Matthew, it's what Jesus told his disciples to do: "Go therefore and *make disciples* of all nations, baptizing them in the name of the Father and of the Son and of the Holy Spirit, teaching them to observe all that I have commanded you" (Matthew 28:19, emphasis added).

The core of living sent, of living on mission for Jesus, is making disciples. Zane Pratt states it clearly, "At the heart of it all there is one command and one task. The heart of the mission of the church is to make disciples."[32]

But what does it mean to make a disciple? To make a disciple is to lead someone from death to life (evangelism) and teach them to grow to become more like Christ (discipleship). But the message for both things remains the same—the good news of the gospel. The gospel is not just the gate we walk through to start our relationship with Jesus. It's also the path that we walk on as we deepen our relationship with him. Disciple making is pouring your life into the lives of others, teaching them the Word of God, helping them to love and obey Jesus more fully, and modeling for them a life rooted in and abiding with Jesus.

Discipleship that produces disciple makers is what holds missions strategy together. Think of it this way: If this year you committed to reaching and discipling two people, and you repeated this every year for twenty years, you would reach and disciple a total of forty people. That's amazing! However, if you invested in those same people and then empowered each of them to disciple two other people, thus multiplying your efforts, all of you could potentially reach and disciple more than a million people in that twenty-year time period. Obviously, this idea has its limitations, but it proves a point: the multiplication of disciples is expanding the gospel around the globe. Disciple making is more than addition, it's multiplication.

This is what Paul is encouraging in 2 Timothy 2:1–2. Discipleship is truly discipleship when it is multiplied: "You then, my child, be strengthened by the grace that is in Christ Jesus, and what you have heard from me in the presence of many witnesses entrust to faithful men, who will be able to teach others also."

Sharing the gospel and making new disciples is a part of being a Christian. We are called to both be and make disciples. The noted German pastor Dietrich Bonhoeffer wrote, "Christianity without the living Christ is inevitably Christianity without discipleship, and Christianity without discipleship is always Christianity without Christ."[33]

Reflection: How are you both being discipled and making disciples in your own life? Both are valuable parts of living a healthy Christian life. Be honest and specific as you reflect.

Start Healthy Churches

The natural outworking of evangelism and discipleship is the planting of new churches. As people come to faith and are discipled, these new members of God's family need to be gathered into churches. It's within local churches that real and profound discipleship can happen in community with other believers.

J. D. Payne writes, "Church planting is at the center of God's purposes in redeeming the lost and broadcasting his glory across every dimension of human society and culture."[34] Church planting is not only important for good missions work, it is vital for the mission of God around the world.

The story of the beginning of the church in Philippi is a beautiful example of what God longs to see globally: the planting and flourishing of new churches in places that need healthy churches.

GROUP DISCUSSION: In your groups or cohorts, have participants read the passages below about the founding of the church in Philippi, which are listed in their books. For each passage, groups should briefly discuss this question: How do you see God establishing and growing his church at this point in the story?

- *Lydia's conversion (Acts 16:11–15)*
- *The jailer's conversion (Acts 16:25–34)*
- *The church started (Acts 16:40)*

The book of Philippians is an outworking of Acts 16. God started a church through the evangelization and discipleship of Lydia, the jailer, and their households. The call of the church today is to be active in planting new and healthy churches that continue the movement of evangelism, discipleship, and church planting.

LESSON 6: LIVING SENT
PREPARATION AND INSTRUCTIONS

As you prepare for this lesson, it may be helpful to consider what the common challenges are for people in your context. What prevents people (yourself included) from living sent?

You may also consider preparing a short, real-life example from your own life to share with the group during the section of the lesson that presents "Practical Ways to Live Sent." The best examples are concise (not overly detailed or long), reveal your need at appropriate levels (not oversharing), and also reveal how God meets that need.

For supplies, you will need to provide one sheet of blank paper, and perhaps something to write with, for each participant. This will be for the Gospel Map activity at the end of the lesson.

LEARNING OBJECTIVES

- To lay a theological foundation based on John 20:21 that every believer is called to "live sent," making Jesus known wherever we live, work, and play

- To teach the concept of missional living, which is living on mission in the everyday rhythms of life: (1) define and explore the concept of missional living, (2) explain the importance of *word* and *deed* ministry, and (3) give practical ways to live out the gospel, in word and deed, in everyday life

- To learn the Gospel Map, a tool for sharing the gospel with others

LESSON CONTENT

The article you read for class laid the foundation that every follower of Jesus is sent. Every Christian is by nature sent out with the gospel. Let's read back over John 20:19–22 and remind ourselves of this core truth.

> On the evening of that day, the first day of the week, the doors being locked where the disciples were for fear of the Jews, Jesus came and stood among them and said to them, "Peace be with you." When he had said this, he showed them his hands and his side. Then the disciples were glad when they saw the Lord. Jesus said to them again, "Peace be with you. As the Father has sent me, even so I am sending you." And when he had said this, he breathed on them and said to them, "Receive the Holy Spirit."

In light of this reality, what does it mean to live our lives as sent people making Jesus known to those around us? *Our call as witnesses for Jesus is a call to live out the gospel in the everyday rhythms of our lives.* This means that sharing Jesus with others must be more than just evangelistic events and encounters. Evangelism does include these, but it's more. It's a call to live a missional life.

Missional living means to take on the posture, practices, and habits of a missionary in the everyday rhythms of life. It means Christ is an ordinary part of your language and actions. Our evangelism is incomplete if it is nothing more than an activity or duty. Simply doing missions is a limited perspective. We are called to be missional—to have the gospel woven into our daily language and actions.

Thomas Hale writes, "No one can say: 'Since I'm not called to be a missionary, I do not have to evangelize my friends and neighbors.' There is no difference, in spiritual terms, between a missionary witnessing in his hometown and a missionary witnessing in Kathmandu, Nepal. We are all called to go—even if it is only to the next room, or the next block. We are all called to be Christ's witnesses by word and deed."[35]

As we consider what it means to have our identities shaped by Christ, living as beloved sent ones, we also have to consider the reality in the world today that location does matter. More people need to go to the people groups, cities, and corners of our world that have little or no access to the gospel. The call to live missionally is not a knock against cross-cultural missions; it's the first step to seeing the gospel go to the ends of the earth.

It's wonderful to hear stories of Christians who embrace this concept and begin to share Jesus and make disciples in their everyday lives.

GROUP DISCUSSION: Instruct groups to take time, as a cohort, to read aloud the testimonies of Christians living on mission in their everyday lives (included in the participant section), and then discuss the following questions:

- *What themes or patterns do you notice from these stories of people living their life on mission?*

- *What potential barriers are these people having to overcome to make Jesus known?*

- *From these examples, what could you apply to your own life?*

Practical Ways to Live Sent

For too long, we have made sharing our faith a duty of the Christian life that only a few participate in. When we do this, we are misunderstanding what sharing Jesus is intended to be. If we will make Jesus and the things of God an ordinary part of our language, conversation, stories, and actions, evangelism will become a joyful lifestyle instead of a task we rarely do. Remember, living on mission is about the rhythm of your life being renewed by God and then moving out to the lives of others. Living on mission (being sent) is a part of whom God has created you to be. As we live life on mission, and as we grow in understanding our own need for God, we'll be ready to share with others. Here are a few ways you might live on mission in the everyday rhythms of your life:[36]

- **Share meals with non-Christians.** You have to eat, so use these moments to slow down and share meals with people who don't yet know God. Nothing breaks down barriers and helps people be vulnerable like eating a meal together. Sharing meals with others is a form of hospitality; it demonstrates that you genuinely care. Jesus shared meals with others as a common ministry practice.

- **Be a regular, learn names, and build relationships.** We live in a world of variety and ease. We could do our shopping online, through a self-checkout, or at a different store every day. Instead, why not go to the same places on a regular basis? When you go, learn people's names and build real relationships. Show that you truly care, and make Jesus known every chance you get through both what you say and how you love. In these moments of relationship, have the courage to speak about Jesus and the life he offers.

- **Get to know your neighbors and share life with them.** Take the time to meet the people who live near you, and learn their names and stories. Find ways to step into their lives every chance you get. Walk the neighborhood regularly and look for opportunities to have conversations. Ask questions, hear and share stories, step into need, and invite people into your life. Open your home for meals and parties. Simply put, see your place of residence as a place of ministry. Build life rhythms that give you a chance to share life with people and make Jesus known.

- **Join in what's going on around you.** Your neighborhood, city, and workplace are full of life. Discover activities and events where you can jump in and play an active role. Too often in the Christian world, we create our own activities and hope non-Christians will join us. Let's flip the script. Join in with what's happening around you. Have a favorite hobby? Find a group in your city and join in with others. Need to get in shape? Join the local gym or a city sports league. Part of living missionally is getting out of our Christian circles to make time to be with those who do not yet know Jesus. Joining in with activities around you is a great way to make this happen.

GROUP DISCUSSION: *Instruct participants to briefly discuss, within their cohorts or as a group, this question: What could you do to make Jesus known to others in the everyday parts of your life? Be specific.*

As we seek to live out some of these missional rhythms, remember these core principles of living with gospel intentionality:

- Use your normal rhythms of life to meet new people and become friends.

- Watch, pray, and listen to the Holy Spirit to discern where God is at work around you.

- Look for ways to boldly and humbly proclaim the gospel to others in word and deed, including sharing your own need and how God is actively working in your own life.[37]

- Remember to consider the context and culture as you share the gospel with others.

Sharing Jesus

As we engage with the gospel regularly in our own lives—repenting, yielding, trusting, and forgiving—it will begin to infuse our language and impact the way we engage with people. As we do this, opportunities to share the gospel will become more evident. *But how do you share the gospel well?*

Sometimes we have just a moment to share a gospel truth and other times we have the opportunity to share a full gospel message and invite people to follow Jesus. The most important thing in sharing the gospel is simply to share. Step out in faith, open your mouth, and talk about Jesus. The Spirit is at work in you. He will guide you as you speak words of truth to others.

It can also be helpful to start with a framework—a skeleton on which you build your gospel. One of these is **Listen, Share, Tell.**

LISTEN TO THEIR STORY—SHARE YOUR STORY—TELL GOD'S STORY

This simple framework encourages you to start with listening. Ask questions of people, listen to their life stories, and be present. See how God is already at work in the person's life. After hearing from them, ask if you can share your story—your testimony of how you came to faith. *Remember that your goal here isn't to celebrate your past sins but to clearly demonstrate your brokenness and need for salvation. Share how, through God's grace, you turned from your sin to God eternal mercy in Jesus. Be sure to include where you currently are struggling and sinning—and how you come to Christ to meet these needs. In essence, you're "preaching the gospel to yourself" and just inviting the other person to listen in on the conversation.* Since you have listened to their story, you can find places to connect your story with theirs. As your story comes to an end, find a place you can move from your testimony and connect it to the story of God, the gospel. This threefold storytelling method allows you to build real relationships with people and invite others to see a living love relationship with God—your relationship with God. These three steps may happen in one setting or may take place over several meetings, listening and sharing as you build relationship with others.

Another way to share the gospel is through the **Gospel Map**, a simple picture used to unpack the gospel.[38]

In the Gospel Map, three pictures serve as markers to tell the whole story of God: kingdom, cross, and grace. There are at least two ways to use the map: (1) as a way to share the gospel story with others or (2) as a way to tell the whole-Bible story of God's redemption from Genesis to Revelation. As you learn the Gospel Map and prepare to use it, here's an encouragement: just relax! You know the gospel because it is at work in your own life. Just share what you know and use the Gospel Map as a guide. Read it, learn it, practice it, and then apply it. Use it to share the gospel story in your own words. This is not a "magic bullet," but a simple way to help remind you of the key truths you need to communicate when sharing the gospel with others. You got this!

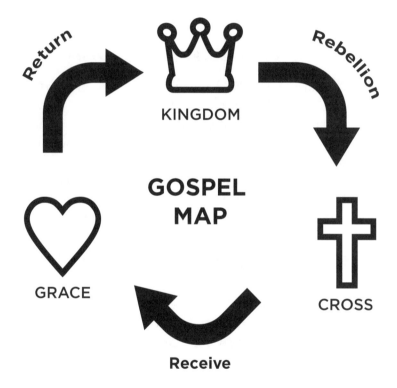

Follow along in your book as we work through each item in the Gospel Map.

KINGDOM. The story of the Bible begins with God. God is the Creator and King of the universe. We were created to experience life with him under his loving rule and reign. Life was originally perfect and satisfying in his kingdom.

REBELLION. Like Adam and Eve, the first man and woman, each of us have rebelled against God's rule and reign, setting ourselves up as rulers of our own lives. Our rebellion results in a broken relationship with God, a broken world, and God's judgment on sin. From Genesis 3 onward, men and women have chosen to rebel against God and his kingdom. We have all agreed with the writer of Judges 17:6, who wrote, "Everyone did what was right in his own eyes." We have turned away God to do what seems right to us. Romans 6:23 tells us that rebellion against God leads to death: "For the wages of sin [rebellion] is death." No matter how are we try, we can't fix this problem ourselves.

CROSS. God knew our problem and sent help. Out of his deep love for us, God sent his own Son to save us. The gospel of God's cross is the good news that through the life, death, and resurrection of Jesus we can be made right with God. The death that we deserved was paid for us through Jesus's work on the cross. This reality gives each person the opportunity to have a restored relationship with God and experience an abundant life under his rule and reign—abundant life in the here and now, and for all eternity. "For Christ also suffered once for sins, the righteous for the unrighteous, that he might bring us to God" (1 Peter 3:18). No matter what you have done, or how far you feel from God, God's invitation to you is to come to him.

RECEIVE. Knowing who Jesus is and what he has done is not enough. By faith, we must turn from living under our own rule to trust in the work of Jesus alone as our only hope for a restored relationship with God. This is how we receive the gift of salvation and become children of God (John 1:12).

GRACE. God's grace is his kindness and mercy toward those who have rebelled against him. God's grace means we are not saved through right answers (Bible knowledge), religious devotion (going to church, etc.), respectable living (morality), or any other self-made righteousness. The appropriate response to what Jesus did on the cross is to turn from our sinful rebellion and to trust that Jesus lived a perfect life on our behalf and suffered the punishment we deserve—to turn from sin and embrace Jesus.

RETURN. Receiving the gospel involves both trusting and turning. We trust solely in the work of Jesus, and we turn from trusting in ourselves and from living under our own rule. The Bible calls this act of returning *repentance*. The gospel invites us to return to living under God's good rule and reign. "Truly, truly, I say to you, whoever hears my word and believes him who sent me has eternal life. He does not come into judgment, but has passed from death to life" (John 5:24).

JOINING THE KINGDOM. The good news of the gospel is not just that we are saved *from* our sin, but also that we are saved *for* living and pursuing God's kingdom and God's purposes (Matthew 6:33). Eternal life isn't solely about going to heaven, but also about knowing, enjoying, and living for God in the here and now.

The message of the Bible demands a response. We have all rebelled against God our King and tried to create our own kingdom. This rebellion will only lead to death. God's invitation to you today is to believe in what he has done for you, through the death and resurrection of Jesus, and to enter into his kingdom. God is inviting you to come to him, to embrace forgiveness, and to know that you are loved and accepted into his kingdom.

> For the wages of sin is death, but the free gift of God is eternal life in Christ Jesus our Lord. (Romans 6:23)

> "For God so loved the world, that he gave his only Son, that whoever believes in him should not perish but have eternal life. For God did not send his Son into the world to condemn the world, but in order that the world might be saved through him." (John 3:16–17)

Our world and our lives are broken. But God, our gracious King, came and made a way for life to become right again. Those who respond to this reality by trusting in God, and turning away from their rebellion, are given new life. They are brought into a relationship with God and now live under his good rule and reign.

INVITATION. Are you ready to turn away from your rebellion and trust in Jesus and in his life, death, and resurrection? If so, he is inviting you to come to him. Jesus tells us in Matthew 11:28–29, "Come to me, all who labor and are heavy laden, and I will give you rest. Take my yoke upon you, and learn from me, for I am gentle and lowly in heart, and you will find rest for your souls."

If you want to give your life to Jesus and trust in what he has done on your behalf, consider the following:

- Take time to come to God and have an honest conversation with him. Admit that you're messed up, broken, and in need of saving. Tell God you have sinned and rebelled against his rule and reign in your life. Embrace the reality that there is nothing you can do to save yourself.

- In light of these things, give your life to God and trust in what Jesus has done for you. Commit to a life fully given to him, living under his good rule and reign.

WHAT'S NEXT. When you turn from your sin and embrace a life found in Jesus, you not only join his good kingdom, you are invited into his family. You become a child of God and a brother or sister with those in the church. If you have become a Christian today, one of your first steps is to find a healthy local church to be a part of. It's a place to grow as a Christian and live in community with others.

GROUP ACTIVITY: Instruct participants to take a sheet of paper and practice sharing the gospel with a partner using the Gospel Map. They should take five minutes each. Tell them, "Don't stress and don't think you need to know exactly what to say. If you are a follower of Jesus, you have experienced the gospel. Simply use the tool to help you tell the story."

LESSON 7: UNDERSTANDING CULTURE

PREPARATION AND INSTRUCTIONS

Instruct participants to gather as usual in groups or cohorts for discussion before the lesson begins.

LEARNING OBJECTIVES

- To define culture and learn why crossing cultures is important to life and ministry

- To understand that everyone has a culture and that no culture is more valuable than another

- To introduce the concepts of culture shock, ethnocentrism, and contextualization

- To give students an understanding of how to be a learner of culture, and tips for crossing cultures effectively

LESSON CONTENT

Let's start at the beginning. **What is culture?** Culture is the word used to describe **how a group of people think, act, and engage in the world.** Culture is the norms and values a particular group of people hold. The missiologist Scott Moreau writes, "Every human being is to a large extent a product of cultural values. God has designed people as learning beings, and the rules of culture that people learn while growing up provide maps that they use to interpret the world around them. No human being escapes culture."[39]

The concept of culture can be used in a variety of ways. At a larger level, we can talk about French or American culture. But we can also talk about Parisian culture or the culture of North Africans living in the diaspora, outside of their home countries. At a micro level, it can refer to more specific cultures created in neighborhoods and within families.

Culture is the way a group of people see and engage the world. It is the sum of their distinctive habits and ways of living.

Everyone has a culture. In fact, our culture is a hodgepodge of the different environments and distinctive cultural values we have experienced throughout our lives. Let's examine this reality through a quote from the author of *You Are Sent*, Nathan Sloan.

> I was born and raised in a family from the southern part of the United States, but our family was distinctly Appalachian.

I was raised in a single-parent family that moved to four different states as I grew up. For college, I moved into the urban core of Chattanooga, Tennessee, experiencing the realities of the city for the first time. After college, I became a pastor in a small rural church in Tennessee. I was once again plopped right back into small-town America. After a few years, I moved to a Kathmandu, Nepal, where I experienced a new level of poverty and city density. I was exposed to other expressions of Christianity and ways of understanding the world. Finally, I moved to Louisville, Kentucky, where our family bought a home in a predominantly African American community and began raising a family in a multicultural environment. Collectively these communities, experiences, and cultures have shaped me into who I am.

Although many of us identify with one primary culture, your individual culture is actually the product of the many different cultures you encounter and engage with in your life.

Let's stop for a moment and think about our own culture. Before we can ever think about crossing another culture well, we need to be able to understand our own culture. Ask yourself, how do you see and engage the world around you? What do you value and how do you think the world should work? Remember, the first step to learning how to effectively cross a culture is to understand your own culture.

PERSONAL REFLECTION: Instruct participants to take a few minutes to think about aspects of their own culture. Ask them to briefly write down answers to the following questions:

- *What are some cultural features of (1) your country, (2) your region, and (3) your family?*

- *Which of these cultural distinctives have especially shaped you?*

- *How might these cultural distinctives vie for your allegiance to the culture of Christ's kingdom as expressed in Scripture? Can you think of a specific example from your life, or in the culture of your country, region, or family?*

Ethnocentrism: Right, Wrong, and Different

Let's think critically about our own culture so we can understand that *there is no right culture*. Let's remember that God was the creator of culture and he finds value and beauty in cultural diversity. Within every culture there are things to celebrate and things to lament, elements of dignity and depravity, things that bring God honor and things that dishonor who he is and who he has called us to be.

We need to be mindful about what we assume is right or wrong in any given culture, especially our own. When we evaluate these cultural differences in light of Scripture, it becomes clear that Christ's kingdom radically reframes the values and virtues of every fallen human culture. At times we'll see that cultural difference aren't really an issue of right or wrong according to biblical values. They are just expressing our human *preferences*. But at other times what seemed like a neutral preference turns out to be rooted more deeply in our sinful hearts. As believers our primary loyalty must always be to Christ and his kingdom, not our country, region, and families. Even the good things about our culture can become idolatrous when we begin to value them above our allegiance to Christ and the things he values the most.

In a fallen world, division and hostility readily develop between people with differing cultural values. But Paul reminds us that true unity, rooted in our primary identity in Christ, can only happen through the power of the gospel at work in us. In Ephesians 2:11–33, he gives us a powerful example of how Jews and Gentiles have been bound together in Christ, being made into one people: "For he himself is our peace, who has made us both one and has broken down in his flesh the dividing wall of hostility by abolishing the law of commandments expressed in ordinances, that he might create in himself one new man in place of the two, so making peace, and might reconcile us both to God in one body through the cross, thereby killing the hostility" (Ephesians 2:14–17).

Under the power of the gospel, the dividing wall of cultural animosity (among other types of division) is laid to waste. Individuals, families, and whole groups can experience unity and fellowship with one another. What Christ did for us on the cross allows us to be united as the body of Christ.

Sounds simple, right? It's not. One reason the vision of unity remains hard to embrace within the church is that cultural distinctives remain. Just because two groups are made one through the gospel does not mean one new culture emerges. Yes, as the church we now all find our citizenship in God's kingdom, but that eternal kingdom remains diverse (Revelation 7:9–10). Being unified across cultural and ethnic distinctives means more than simply pushing the hardship away, more than pretending hurts and wounds don't exist. No, true unity calls us to push *into* hardships with our brothers and sisters who live, think, and act differently than we do. We are called to set down our preferences, be it ever so hard, and fight for unity in diversity. This is a hard road to walk—near impossible without the power of the gospel at work in our lives and in our churches.

The gospel not only compels us to defer our cultural preferences to be united with Christians who are different from us. It also allows us to die to ourself, repenting of our own misplaced allegiances and embracing kingdom values, so that we can cross cultures and bring the gospel to those without Jesus. This may be to a culturally distinct neighborhood in your city, to a refugee camp in sub-Saharan Africa, or to a megacity in Asia. The location may differ but the difficulty remains. To cross a culture well, we need to wrestle with our cultural arrogance and die to our preferences for the good of others.

The attitude of "my culture is right" is a universal condition. This is called **ethnocentrism**, the idea that your culture and way of life are best, that the way you understand and engage the world is the right way, with the result that you see other cultures as inferior or wrong.[40] Ethnocentrism may sound harsh, but we are all ethnocentric to some degree.

GROUP DISCUSSION: Instruct participants to discuss the following questions in their cohorts or groups:

- *What specific examples of ethnocentrism do you see in your culture and in yourself?*

- *What are specific ways in which you can push against your ethnocentrism and effectively love those from other cultures and other ways of thinking?*

Adjustment and Culture Shock

When we think about stepping into the lives of those from other cultures, we often think of getting on a plane and stepping off in some far-flung place across the world. Yes, this is an essential aspect of crossing cultures, but most of us naturally cross cultures every day.

Let's consider what an ordinary day in the life of someone crossing cultures could look like.

Coffee shop. On her way to work in downtown Atlanta, Katherine visits a coffee shop in a trendy part of town with distinct cultural expectations of how she should interact with others. She was expected to order a certain way, and there were unspoken rules for where she sat and the proper interactions with those in the coffee shop. Katherine found herself interacting with people of different ethnicities, nationalities, and streams of life.

Car mechanic. After work, Katherine had a flat tire and stopped by an auto-body shop on the outskirts of her community. The men who helped with her flat tire were a bit rough, yet very kind. There was a clear culture in the shop including a distinct vocabulary and cultural interactions. The language and cultural expectations were different from her normal pattern of life.

International friends. That evening, Katherine went to dinner in the home of her Cuban friend, Marie. Marie is a faithful follower of Jesus who has been friends with Katherine for years. Marie is from Havana, raised in Miami, educated in Boston, and now living in Atlanta. Although Katherine and Marie share a love for Cuban food and music, the way Marie views life and interacts with the world is very different. Yet despite these differences, they gladly cross cultural distinctives and maintain a beautiful friendship.

This was a day in the life of a fictitious character, but I bet you can recount similar situations in your own life. Multiple times a day, we are forced to use our developed skills to understand, interpret, and effectively cross cultures and cultural distinctives. Learning to cross cultures effectively is a needed skill for everyone, whether they live overseas or not.

GROUP DISCUSSION: *Instruct participants to think about their own lives, and recall a time they recognized cultural differences around them and then adjusted. They should share within their group how they have done this well—or done it poorly.*

Crossing cultures is a combination of funny experiences, embarrassment, and hard work. Effective cross-cultural ministry does not just happen. It's a learned skill that takes effort and practice.

Crossing cultures often causes us to experience something called **culture shock**. Thomas Hale, former medical missionary to Nepal, defines culture shock as a "sense of disorientation, together with the uneasiness and anxiety that such disorientation produces."[41] He writes elsewhere that culture shock is "like a game in which you are always one point behind. The only way to win is to join the other side."[42]

Culture shock happens when we become disoriented to the rules of life around us. We enter a situation assuming we know how to interact, but we soon realize we are confused and out of place. That feeling of lostness and anxiety is culture shock. Culture shock isn't a sign that you're a bad missionary or haven't crossed cultures well. It's an inevitable part of experiencing the differences in a new culture. The important thing is how you respond to culture shock. Culture shock only abates when we either flee a situation or we choose to press in and learn the new culture in which God has placed us.

GROUP DISCUSSION: *Instruct participants to read the culture-shock case study in their books and discuss it within their group, using the questions at the end of the case study.*

Culture Matters

Culture is a foundational idea that helps shape not only ministry, but life itself. We all come from a culture. We all value and live out a culture. And we are all having to cross the boundaries of culture every day. For a Christian living on mission, it is essential to cross cultures effectively to make Jesus known. We do this by being learners, asking questions, making genuine friendships, and living out of a posture of humility toward others.

Let us be Christians who are committed to learning, valuing, and cross cultures well. Let us be known as a people who both love God and love people from every culture.

LESSON 8: STATE OF THE WORLD

PREPARATION AND INSTRUCTIONS

Illustration. If you want to use the bean illustration during the lesson, prepare a clear jar filled with 7,500 beans for each group or cohort. Paint just one bean a distinctive color to represent the one person in 7,500 who is a Christian believer in Istanbul. Make sure the container is big enough for people to put their hands in. Consider using northern or pinto beans. Each one-pound bag has about 4,500 to 4,800 beans in it. You could also do this with 15,000 beans and paint two of the beans to represent the number of Christians in the city. The benefit to this is that you could emphasize the difficulty of finding community with other believers because Christians are so few.

Cross-Cultural Missionary. Arrange to have a cross-cultural missionary share in class (virtually or in person) about their life and ministry overseas. If your church does not personally know a cross-cultural missionary, reach out to area churches or a mission agency that can connect you with a missionary.

Beforehand, ask the missionary to share about their personal experience in their ministry context. It's important that participants hear real-life stories from the field that reflect limitations, dependence on God, and genuine vulnerability. Keep this time with a missionary to fifteen minutes so that there is enough time to complete the lesson. Consider asking your visiting missionary to answer the following questions, or something similar:

- How did God lead you into cross-cultural missions?

- What have been some significant struggles you've experienced while on the field, and how did God meet you in those struggles?

- How have you experienced God's love in your own life and ministry?

- What advice or encouragement would you give someone who is exploring a call to go into global missions?

LEARNING OBJECTIVES

- To become more aware of the significant lostness of the world through the lens of world population, people groups, and urbanization

- To grow hope for God's work among the unreached and forgotten places and peoples of the world

- To consider how we can engage with the enormous gospel need of our world

LESSON CONTENT

Let's begin our time together with a personal story from our author:

> Having been in missions for a long time, I've been blessed to travel to some unbelievable places to visit missionaries and encourage and international church leaders. Each time I land in a new city and spend time with Christians, I am deeply encouraged. Yet my trip to Istanbul opened my eyes in a new way.
>
> For years, I'd heard stories from a young man in my local church who lives and serves in Istanbul, Turkey. He often told me that Istanbul is a massive city divided between Europe and Asia, with a mix of cultures and in desperate need of the gospel. He was so passionate for his city that his passion was bleeding over into my heart. When I landed and walked out of the airport, I was instantly broken over the city.
>
> With a population of more than sixteen million, Istanbul is one of the largest cities in the world. It was once a

stronghold for the Christian faith. But now Islam, and to a lesser degree secularism, dominate life there. In 2010, writing about the country of Turkey as whole, *Operation World* painted a bleak but realistic picture of the country's lostness: "For over 1,000 years the region was a bastion of Christendom, but it later became a strong propagator of Islam. The Christian population has declined from 22% to 0.21% [less in Istanbul] since 1900. Only 0.008% of people in Turkey are evangelical."[43] Did you hear that? Only about one-hundredth of a percent of the people in Turkey and Istanbul are evangelical believers.

Recently, the number of Christians has increased and God is moving through his church in Turkey. But the numbers are still shockingly small. One ministry, The Silas Project (also known as Friends of Turkey), estimates the total number of Protestant evangelicals in Turkey to be around 7,300 and growing.[44] This is out of a total population in Turkey of eighty-four million people.

This staggering reality hit home for me toward the end of my trip. A few of us decided to visit the top of the largest building in Istanbul. As I overlooked the city from the roof, I could see far in every direction. To the one side was water, and to the other was the city as far as I could see. The massive population hit me hard. On that roof, I got a glimpse of what sixteen million people densely packed together looks like. I began to wonder how many of these people actually knew Jesus as Savior. I turned to the young missionary from our church and asked, "How many Protestant, evangelical Christians do you think live in the city?" He looked back at me with brokenness and said, "Around two thousand evangelical Christians live in this city." Two thousand out of sixteen million. Later he reminded me that more Christians gather in just a few churches on a Sunday in my home city of Louisville, Kentucky, than do in all of Istanbul. That reality has stuck with me.

What I saw in Istanbul is a picture into our world today: individuals, cities, and whole people groups need to experience the hope and life that only come through knowing Jesus.

The Lostness of Our World

We live in a big world. *Really* big. So big, in fact, that it's hard to wrap our minds around both the size of the population and the contours of the various cultures and people groups.

In 1950, the world's population was 2.5 billion people. As of 2022, the population was roughly eight billion. The world's population has tripled in the last seventy years. What does that even mean? How can we get our minds around such a large and incomprehensible number as eight billion people?

Think about it this way: There are sixty seconds in a minute. That's a concept and a number we all understand. So let's count five seconds together . . . 1, 2, 3, 4, 5.

Now, to better understand a number like eight billion, imagine each person is represented by a second. How long would it take to count every person on earth? Any guesses? If we started right now and didn't stop, it would take 254 years!

The growth of the world's population is staggering. Every year an estimated 140 million people are born.[45] That's the population of Russia being born into our world every year.[46] With staggering growth like this, it is easy to understand the urgent need to share the gospel with others, make new disciples, and plant new churches. Not only do we need to share the gospel with others, we need to go to places where people have little to no access to the gospel.

Out of the current 8 billion people on earth, roughly 660 million are evangelical Christians.[47] That's just 8.25 percent of the world population. Meaning roughly 92 percent of people are not evangelical followers of Jesus. This doesn't mean we know that's how many people are truly followers of Jesus, because we do not know the hearts of people, and we don't fully comprehend all that God is doing in the world.

In the last few years, the term "evangelical" has been distorted and lost much of its historical meaning. In this lesson, by the term "evangelical," we are referring to a broad movement of churches and Christians who hold to salvation by grace through faith in Christ alone, an authoritative and infallible view of the Bible, and are committed to the proclamation of the gospel.

These statistics are limited in scope but it does show that a large portion of the world has yet to follow Jesus as Savior, with many having little to no access to the gospel. Meaning that even if a person wanted to learn more about Jesus or the Christian faith, they would have no Bible in their language to read or no Christian to talk to.

The task of the Great Commission is truly more enormous than we can fathom—and yet so is the One who commissions us to go.

People Groups

Another way to think about the lostness of our world is through the lens of people groups. A people group is an ethnic group of people with a distinct language and culture that sets them apart from other groups. According to a leading research group, there are around 9,800 distinct people groups on earth.[48] One way to think of a people group is that it is the largest group within which the gospel can spread without facing significant barriers of understanding and acceptance due to language, culture, and geography.[49]

The call to the church through the Great Commission is to see disciples made and multiplied among every people group on earth, so how are we doing? A people group is considered unreached when the indigenous community of Christians within the group is unable to engage their own people and plant churches in a substantial way. Unreached does not mean there are no Christians within a people group, but rather that there are not enough Christians to effectively reach their own people with the gospel. Often this is understood as having fewer than 2 percent evangelical Christians within a people group (although others would advocate for a more nuanced understanding of the term unreached).

With that understanding, of the more than 9,800 people groups on earth, 4,400 of them would be unreached.[50] The task at hand is massive. Some of these unreached people groups are twenty to thirty million people in size, and some groups are far smaller. The total number of people in unreached groups globally is more than three billion.[51]

As we've mentioned in other lessons, your mission as a believer is to reach people with the gospel both where you are *and* onward toward the nations (where you are and where you're not). For the nations to know and worship Jesus as Savior, it will take more disciple-making Christians learning new languages and new cultures, moving to unreached places among unreached and forgotten peoples.

Although it is healthy and needed to understand global missions from more than just the people group lens, it is one of the essential perspectives that gives the church clarity in missions engagement and helps drive the mission forward.

Cities

Yet another way to grasp lostness is to understand the growing urbanization of our world. More than 50 percent of the world's population now lives in cities. According to the United Nations, almost 180 thousand people move to cities across the world every day. That's nearly 5.5 million people a month or a new San Francisco Bay area created every thirty days.[52]

Like the population of our world, the size and scope of cities can be hard to comprehend. Let's think back to Istanbul, Turkey.

GROUP ACTIVITY: If you prepared jars of beans, direct participants to their group's jar, and explain: "This is a jar with approximately 8,000 beans in a container that represents the 16 million people that live in Istanbul, Turkey. To better understand the scope of lostness in this city, we painted one bean to represent the total number of Christ followers in the city. That's one Christian for every 8,000 people! Take a moment to look in the jar, put your hands in it, and move the beans around. As you see and experience this picture of lostness, what are you thinking and feeling?"

This growing urban reality has a huge impact on how our world functions and how we seek to reach people with the gospel. If we are going to truly be effective in seeing the world know and love Jesus, we must take the city seriously. Al Mohler drives this point home when he writes, "In the course of less than 300 years, our world will have shifted from one in which only 3 percent of people live in cities, to one in which 80 percent are resident in urban areas. If the Christian church does not learn new models of urban ministry, we will find ourselves on the outside looking in. The Gospel of Jesus Christ must call a new generation of committed Christians into these teeming cities."[53]

The city represents a new opportunity for reaching the nations of the earth. Unreached people groups from around the world are moving to cities for jobs or education, to flee violence, or for any number of other reasons. Engaging cities with the gospel allows us to have access to the unreached like never before. This does not mean language and cultural barriers do not need to be crossed, but the unreached are more accessible and at times more open to spiritual conversations.

God Is at Work

As we look at the statistics and wrestle with the reality of global lostness, it would be easy to get overwhelmed and lose perspective. With so many individuals and people groups without Jesus, is there any hope? Yes!

The task God gave us as his people, the church, is a task that *he* will complete. He is the initiator, sustainer, and finisher of the Great Commission. We have more than a faint hope. God has promised that he will complete his work. Let's look to Revelation 7:9–10 to see this promise fulfilled. "After this I looked, and behold, a great multitude that no one could number, from every nation, from all tribes and peoples and languages, standing before the throne and before the Lamb, clothed in white robes, with palm branches in their hands, and crying out with a loud voice, 'Salvation belongs to our God who sits on the throne, and to the Lamb!'"

What God starts he finishes. But how is God making his name known among the lost? He is using his global church.

There are more evangelical Christians alive today than ever before. Evangelical Christianity is currently the fastest growing religion in the world, growing twice as fast as Islam and three times as fast as the global population.[54] Simply put, God is building his church.

Although the church in the West is either stagnating or declining, the church in other parts of the world is growing. Christians in Asia, Africa, and Latin America now make up the majority of the global church.[55] Some estimate that up to 70 percent of the world's Bible-believing Christians (as opposed to nominal or cultural Christians) now live in the non-Western world.[56]

Although the highest percentage of unreached people groups still lie within Asia, the church there continues to grow rapidly—from 22 million in 1900 to 370 million in 2005.[57] Not only is the church growing, often under intense persecution, but the church in Asia has become one of the leaders in missionary sending. The same is true in Africa and Latin America. These regions have growing churches and growing missionary movements. Christianity has become the majority religion in Africa, and the African church has sent an estimated 13,000 cross-cultural missionaries.[58] Much could also be said about the staggering growth of believers and missionaries sent from the Latin American church. Missions has changed. Missions used to be seen as "from the West to the rest," but now it is better described as a movement from everywhere to everywhere.

What does all this mean for us? Jason Mandryk puts it well: "There is much to celebrate in our generation, but we temper this with the reality that billions of people—from thousands of different people groups—have not yet had an opportunity to worship the Lord Jesus, or even hear about him in a meaningful way."[59] The task before us is overwhelming, but our God has promised to finish his mission. And he has given us a role to play. Let me ask you: **How will you invest your life in seeing the nations come to know and worship Jesus?**

LESSON 9: YOUR PLACE IN GOD'S GLOBAL MISSION

PREPARATION AND INSTRUCTIONS

All of the lessons so far have been building to this lesson on application: What role do participants have in expanding God's global kingdom? The structure of this class will be a bit different. The teaching portion will be shorter (only about thirty minutes) and will be followed by two key application exercises. Both will require thoughtful preparation from you, the leader.

"Ways to Live Sent" Opportunities

This in-class exercise will offer participants pathways for taking a next step in missions. You will spend time presenting clear and accessible opportunities for them to get more deeply involved in missions both locally and globally. Before class, collect resources and contact information for many different ministries in your church and local area that you can share with your group. From this, create a list of many pathways your local church would support, customized based on what missions your church is involved in, your church's local context, and the maturity of those in the class. Make some opportunities local, others regional or national, and still others global. Make sure some pathways are easily accessible while others require further development and discernment. Try to have a mix of short-term (weeks), mid-term (months) and long-term (years) opportunities. You may find it helpful to connect with sending agencies your church partners with already in order to find out what opportunities are available. Offer to meet with people to help them process and explore their next step.

Here are some examples of categories of pathways you could offer your people:

- Give clear ways to share Jesus and make disciples **where people live, work, and play**. This could happen through further training and encouragement to share Jesus in their neighborhood, in their workplace, or with family members. Consider emphasizing the

Gospel Map found in lesson 6 or another evangelism tool. More than anything, encourage people to adopt a missional lifestyle.

- Share ways to serve in **local missions** through your church and in area ministries. Consider connecting people to tangible service opportunities in outreach programs and with vetted area ministries.

- Highlight **short-term trips** your local church is taking. Taking a short-term trip can be a great way for people to take their next step in living sent and developing the skills they need to do this well.

- Share ways to serve **refugees and international students** in your area.

- Give clear ways to **pray for the nations and care for or support cross-cultural missionaries**. Share online prayer tools and other resources that can equip people to pray well.

- Highlight **domestic church plants** and clear ways to serve and pray.

- Show a clear pathway to being sent as a **mid-term or long-term missionary** from your local church. If possible, share with participants a developed sending process that allows people to take their next step in global missions. This process, or sending pipeline, should include aspects of assessment, development, one-on-one mentorship, and more. For more help in this area, connect with the leaders of the Upstream Collective (theupstreamcollective.org).

"So, What's Next" Exercise

This in-class exercise helps participants debrief their experiences in a personal way. The activity will mirror the opening tear-off sheet activity in lesson 1. Make sure to leave time to do this section well. You will need to provide large sheets of paper on the walls around the classroom or elsewhere, one for each student, clustered according to cohorts if participants are divided that way. Provide markers to use. Or if you prefer, you could also do this exercise using blank sheets of regular-sized paper. The participant section of this book takes participants through the process of completing this activity.

LEARNING OBJECTIVES

- To show how vocational calling is a deep and growing conviction for a specific ministry that is rooted in God and is confirmed through his Word, the Spirit in our lives, and our local church
- To offer pathways into global missions
- To help students see what next step God is calling them to take as a result of this course

LESSON CONTENT

When we talk about calling, we might get confused between the calling we all have as Christians and a specific calling to a vocation or task. God's calling on the life of *every Christian* is to know him, to enjoy him, and to glorify him forever.[60] This calling is about living our lives wholly for God in all we do and making him known to others in how we live and what we say, regardless of our occupation or geographical location.

Yet when we think of *calling* in a missions context, we are often referring to a call *some Christians* have to a specific task, vocation, people, or location. In this lesson, we are going to consider the importance of the calling all Christians share and also look at the specifics of what one person might do with their life and profession as they enjoy God and glorify him forever. We will refer to this second, specific calling as our *vocational calling*.

Discovering our vocational calling is a tricky topic. God often uses multiple means, experiences, and people to help us understand our vocational calling in life. These can include confirmation from Scripture, specific circumstances that lead to open opportunities, growing passion, and affirmation from other trusted Christians in our lives. One thing to keep in mind is that we are unique people, and the way God calls us to himself and his mission are just as unique.

Often, we make the concept of "calling" more mystical than it is intended to be. It's true that God leads and guides us according to his will, but when we start to think we have to *find* God's calling, as if he is hiding it from us, we twist God's intent. We can end up thinking that finding our vocational calling is a test of how strong our faith is or how well we know God. We can even start to believe that difficulties come because we have misunderstood or missed God's vocational calling! Let us be clear: God is not hiding his calling from us.

Before we dive into what exactly a vocational calling or leading to missions looks like, let's explore four helpful insights about it.

1. Vocational calling is best understood in the faithfulness of the everyday. Philip Yancey articulates this well when he writes, "The Bible contains very little specific advice on the techniques of guidance, but very much on the proper way to maintain a love relationship with God."[61] The key to following God's calling in any area of life is found in a love relationship with him, one where we seek to be with him and obey him. As we do this daily, we will be fulfilling the calling he has for us as his children as well as the larger calling we often long to know. Thomas Hale writes, "Don't panic. Just keep moving as far ahead as you see. God will reveal the route to you as you have need. He knows the end; we don't have to."[62]

What a comforting thought! Your job is not to *figure out* God's call for your life but to *follow* him in the everyday, loving him and making his love known. So, if you are longing to know God's vocational calling for your life, faithfully follow God daily and you will be living out his call for you as his child. Remember, "The heart of man plans his way, but the LORD establishes his steps" (Proverbs 16:9). God leads us step-by-step in a loving relationship with him. "Trust in the LORD with all your heart, and do not lean on your own understanding. In all your ways acknowledge him, and he will make straight your paths" (Proverbs 3:5–6).

2. *Calling* can be a loaded word. We romanticize the word to the point where it's unhelpful. *Calling* normally refers to the greater vision or vocation of your life, but its overemphasis in cross-cultural missions has confused people or caused them not to move in obedience toward the nations. The idea of a calling may sound so grand they wonder if they've really received one.

There are other words that can be just as helpful as *calling*, if not more helpful. We can also think about God's *guidance* for us, like a shepherd who guides his sheep day by day. Where is he leading us today and where will he lead us in the future? There is a final destination that the shepherd knows, but our job as sheep is to listen to the shepherd's voice and follow him.

Conviction is another helpful word. The convictions God gives you can help drive you toward the things he would have you invest your life in. What breaks your heart? What moves you? What makes you passionate? If the nations are a growing conviction in your life, it may be that God is guiding you toward global missions.

3. Calling comes in community. A vocational calling to global missions, or to any major life change, should not happen in isolation. Vocational calling happens in community with other Christians, primarily through the local church.

In our Western culture of strong individualism, there is a tendency toward making significant life choices apart from community. But God intends us to root our lives in a local body of believers where we are known and know others. As we live and serve within a local church, our gifts and areas of growth become evident. Our pastors, mentors, and friends help us grow in character, knowledge, and skill for ministry. They speak into our lives and help bring discernment to God's leading in our lives.

4. All are called; some are assigned to vocational ministry. All those who follow Jesus are called to live on mission, and some are given specific assignments for vocational ministry (missionary, church planter, etc.). For example, God calls *everyone* to make Jesus known wherever they live life, and he calls *some* to cross language and cultural boundaries to make disciples.

But again, a vocational call or guidance to a specific ministry does not have to come in a dramatic way. God can use a variety of people, places, and experiences to call us to global missions. We need to fight the tendency to make a call to global missions some mystical experience. It definitely can be, but often God's vocational call comes through ordinary means.

So, what is a vocational call? The book *Encountering Missionary Life and Work* defines it as "an intense conviction that the sovereign God, through the Word, the Holy Spirit, and the community of faith, has set apart a follower of Christ for a participation in a specific ministry."[63] As we examine the Scriptures, we see numerous ways God leads and guides his people. Take time in class (or after class if time does not permit) to read one or more of the following stories of how God led his people:

- Moses (Exodus 3)
- Samuel (1 Samuel 3:8)
- Isaiah (Isaiah 6)
- Jesus's disciples (Matthew 4:20–22)
- Paul and Barnabas (Acts 13:1–4)

God led each of these people, step by step, into a deeper relationship with himself. That is the invitation to us as well: to make knowing God and enjoying a relationship with him primary. If you focus on loving and following God, everything else will fall into place. This doesn't mean you will have an easy journey, but it does mean that God's ultimate purpose (you becoming more like Christ) will occur. And as you become more like Christ, a marker of your spiritual maturity is that you will move out to others with the gospel.

Are you called? Yes, you are called to a life on mission! But are you called to vocational ministry? To cross-cultural ministry? I don't know, but as your local church, we want to help you explore what God is leading you toward. Here are a few general principles for understanding God's leading in your life. These are simple wisdom principles to consider as you reflect upon a possible vocational calling.[64]

1. Do you have an ever-deepening and growing relationship with God?

2. Is the gospel impacting your life regularly? Are you regularly reading Scripture and hearing it preached?

3. Are you talking to God about his call on your life?

4. Are you able to use wisdom and common sense to guide your choices related to your vocational calling?

5. Do you have a personal conviction and desire to do this work?

6. Have you considered what you have learned from your previous experiences and circumstances?

7. Have you sought and gained counsel from the local church and other godly people?

8. Knowing the challenges that may come, do you have peace from the Holy Spirit?

This nine-week course has been building toward one question:

WHAT IS YOUR ROLE IN GOD'S GLOBAL MISSION?

As we consider this question, we might also ask:

WHAT IS YOUR NEXT STEP?

ACKNOWLEDGMENTS

Thank you to all who made this project possible. I'm often reminded that great work rarely happens in isolation. The most helpful ideas come through a community effort that produces more impactful work.

Thank you to the many missions pastors who have helped me flesh out this idea. Thank you to Rebecca Ramirez and Josmel LaFontaine who helped to evaluate, field test, and recreate the content within our local church, Sojourn Church Midtown. Thank you to Ian Galloway, Julissa LaFontaine, and Jack Klumpenhower for their insights and editing work. And finally, I owe a huge debt of gratitude to Serge and especially Margaret-Elliotte Rebello, Marc Davis, and Patric Knaak. The team at Serge invested time and energy to make *You Are Sent* more focused on the heart and gospel renewal.

I pray that God uses our combined efforts to inspire a whole new generation of "sent ones" to bask in the unending love of Jesus and, as a result, to make that love known to others.

ENDNOTES

Glossary

1. Craig Ott and Gene Wilson, *Global Church Planting: Biblical Principles and Best Practices for Multiplication* (Grand Rapids: Baker Academic, 2011), 8.

2. Henry T. Blackaby and Avery T. Willis, *On Mission with God: Living God's Purpose for His Glory* (Nashville: Broadman & Holman, 2002), 3.

3. Claude Hickman, "What Is a People Group?" The Traveling Team, January 30, 2015, http://www.thetravelingteam.org/articles/what-is-a-people-group.

4. Stephen T. Um and Justin Buzzard, *Why Cities Matter: To God, the Culture, and the Church* (Wheaton, IL: Crossway, 2013), 27.

5. Tim Keller, "To Transform a City," website of *Christianity Today*, https://www.christianitytoday.com/pastors/2011/winter/tim-keller-transform-city.html.

6. Gregg R. Allison, *Baker Compact Dictionary of Theological Terms* (Grand Rapids: Baker, 2016), s.v. "wrath."

Lesson 1

1. Craig Ott, Stephen J. Strauss, and Timothy C. Tennent, *Encountering Theology of Mission: Biblical Foundations, Historical Developments, and Contemporary Issues* (Grand Rapids: Baker Academic, 2010), 3.

2. The concept of the church as a sign, instrument, and foretaste of the kingdom comes from Serge missionary Bob Heppe.

Lesson 2

1. Sally Lloyd-Jones, *The Jesus Storybook Bible: Every Story Whispers His Name* (Grand Rapids: Zondervan, 2007), 17.

2. *New Bible Dictionary*, 2nd ed. (Downers Grove, IL: InterVarsity, 1982), s.v. "wrath."

3. Ott, Strauss, and Tennent, *Encountering Theology of Mission*, 331.

Lesson 3

1. Ralph D. Winter, "The Kingdom Strikes Back: Ten Epochs of Redemption History" in *Perspectives on the World Christian Movement: A Reader*, ed. Ralph D. Winter and Steven C. Hawthorne (Pasadena, CA: William Carey, 2013), 209–27.

2. Brad Bell is the author of *The Sending Church Defined*. The quote is from his teaching on missions history at Sojourn Church Midtown in Louisville, Kentucky in 2015.

3. Robert Louis Wilken, *The First Thousand Years: A Global History of Christianity* (New Haven, CT: Yale University Press, 2013), 65–66.

4. Edward L. Smither, *Christian Mission: A Concise Global History* (Bellingham, WA: Lexham Press, 2019), 29–30.

5. Stephen Neill, *A History of Christian Missions, 2nd ed., revised by Owen Chadwick* (London: Penguin, 1990), 44–46.

6. Ruth A. Tucker, *From Jerusalem to Irian Jaya: A Biographical History of Christian Missions* (Grand Rapids: Zondervan, 2004), 21–22.

7. Tucker, 37.

8. Smither, *Christian Mission*, 40.

9. Tucker, *From Jerusalem to Irian Jaya*, 40.

10. Tucker, 40.

11. Ralph Winter, *World Mission: An Analysis of the World Christian Movement*, ed. Jonathan Lewis (Pasadena, CA: William Carey, 1994), 4-16.

Lesson 4

1. Neill, *A History of Christian Missions*, 21–22.

2. John Starke, *The Possibility of Prayer: Finding Stillness with God in a Restless World* (Downers Grove, IL: InterVarsity, 2020), 95–96.

Lesson 5

1. Christopher J. H. Wright, *The Mission of God: Unlocking the Bible's Grand Narrative* (Downers Grove, IL: InterVarsity, 2018), 62.

Lesson 6

1. Robert E. Coleman, *The Master Plan of Evangelism* (Grand Rapids: Revell, 2008), 88.

2. The Gospel Map was created by Luke Skeen, with help from Mike S., for Sojourn Church Midtown in Louisville, Kentucky. It has been adapted and used with permission.

3. Robert N. Bellah et al., *Habits of the Heart: Individualism and Commitment in American Life* (Berkeley, CA: University of California Press, 1996), 142.

Lesson 7

1. Duane Elmer, *Cross-Cultural Connections: Stepping out and Fitting in Around the World* (Downers Grove, IL: InterVarsity, 2002), 45.

2. This parable is found in many publications and online articles including Dave Gibbons's book, *The Monkey and the Fish: Liquid Leadership for a Third-Culture Church* (Grand Rapids: Zondervan, 2009) and *Cross-Cultural Connections* by Duane Elmer. Its original source is unknown.

3. Questions adapted from Elmer, *Cross-Cultural Connections*, 14–15.

4. Press Trust of India, "20 Years after Graham Staines Murder, Accused Nabbed in Odisha," website of *The Hindu*, last modified September 21, 2019, https://www.thehindu.com/news/national/other-states/20-years-after-graham-staines-murder-accused-nabbed-in-odisha/article29480156.ece#.

5. Press Trust of India, "Bible Translated in Oriya Dialect," website of the *Hindustan Times*, November 25, 2006, https://www.hindustantimes.com/india/bible-translated-in-oriya-dialect/story-Kk7xAxiP8nCw9eVXw79cJO.html.

6. "Staines Murder Case: Dara Seeks Review of SC Verdict," website of *The Indian Express*, March 9, 2011, https://indianexpress.com/article/india/latest-news/staines-murder-case-dara-seeks-review-of-sc-verdict/.

7. "Christian Persecution: Statistics & Solutions," Open Doors USA, accessed January 31, 2022, https://www.opendoorsusa.org/christian-persecution/. Data is from the 2021 reporting period.

8. Paul Borthwick and Dave Ripper, *The Fellowship of the Suffering: How Hardship Shapes Us for Ministry and Mission* (Downers Grove, IL: InterVarsity, 2018), 11.

9. Steve Saint, "Sovereignty, Suffering, and the Work of Missions," Desiring God (website), October 8, 2005, https://www.desiringgod.org/messages/sovereignty-suffering-and-the-work-of-missions.

10. Elisabeth Elliot, *Suffering Is Never for Nothing* (Nashville: B&H, 2019), back flap.

Lesson 8

1. Lesslie Newbigin, *Foolishness of the Greeks: The Gospel and Western Culture* (Grand Rapids: Eerdmans, 1999), 124.

Lesson 9

1. John Piper, *Let the Nations Be Glad!: The Supremacy of God in Missions* (Grand Rapids: Baker, 2010), 232.

2. The "So, What's Next" activity has been adapted from an exercise entitled "Winning Hand," created by Chase Abner, Lead Church Planting Catalyst - Iowa, North American Mission Board. Used by permission.

Leader's Notes

1. Lloyd-Jones, *The Jesus Storybook Bible*, 36.

2. A. Scott Moreau, Gary R. Corwin, and Gary B. McGee, *Introducing World Missions: A Biblical, Historical, and Practical Survey* (Grand Rapids: Baker, 2020), 30.

3. Walter C. Kaiser, *Mission in the Old Testament: Israel as a Light to the Nations* (Grand Rapids: Baker, 2009), 20.

4. Kaiser, 9–10.

5. Mark Dever, *The Message of The Old Testament: Promises Made* (Wheaton, IL: Crossway, 2006), 182.

6. Eric E. Wright, *A Practical Theology of Missions: Dispelling the Mystery, Recovering the Passion* (Leominster, UK: Day One, 2010), 58.

7. J. Alec Motyer, *Isaiah: An Introduction and Commentary*, Tyndale Old Testament Commentaries (Downers Grove, IL: InterVarsity, 1999), 311.

8. D. A. Carson, *The Gospel According to John*, Pillar New Testament Commentary (Grand Rapids: Eerdmans, 1991), 216.

9. Ott, Strauss, and Tennent, *Encountering Theology of Mission*, 309–16. Tennent writes in detail how this classic threefold paradigm created by Alan Race in his work, Christians and Religious Pluralism, though helpful, is limited. Tennent provides a more thorough, evangelical understanding of these concepts.

10. Ott, Strauss, and Tennent, 299.

11. Zane Pratt, M. David Sills, and Jeff K. Walters, *Introduction to Global Missions* (Nashville: B&H, 2014), 84–85.

12. Pratt, Sills, and Walters, 85.

13. Smither, *Christian Mission*, xix.

14. This whole section on Zinzendorf and the Moravians has been adapted from Tucker, *From Jerusalem to Irian Jaya*.

15. David A. Schattschneider, "Pioneers in Mission: Zinzendorf and the Moravians," *International Bulletin of Missionary Research*, April 1984, 64.

16. Tucker, *From Jerusalem to Irian Jaya*, 101.

17. William J. Danker, *Profit for the Lord: Economic Activities in Moravian Missions* (Eugene, OR: Wipf and Stock, 1971), 73.

18. Tucker, *From Jerusalem to Irian Jaya*, 100.

19. J. Herbert. Kane, *A Concise History of the Christian World Mission: A Panoramic View of Missions from Pentecost to the Present* (Grand Rapids: Baker, 1978), 85.

20. Tucker, *From Jerusalem to Irian Jaya*, 123. Carey's booklet was titled, An Enquiry into the Obligations of Christians to Use Means for the Conversion of the Heathens.

21. Smither, *Christian Mission*, 110.

22. Lesley Hildreth, "Missionaries You Should Know: George Liele," International Mission Board, June 26, 2018, https://www.imb.org/2018/06/26/missionaries-you-should-know-george-liele/.

23. Smither, *Christian Mission*, xiii.

24. Hildreth, "Missionaries You Should Know: George Liele."

25. Hildreth.

26. Tucker, *From Jerusalem to Irian Jaya*, 186.

27. Tucker, 300–301.

28. Paul Hattaway, "A Captivating Vision," interview by Tim Stafford, website of *Christianity Today*, April 1, 2004, https://www.christianitytoday.com/ct/2004/april/5.84.html.

29. Nour Dados and Raewyn Connell, "The Global South," *American Sociological Association* 11, no. 1 (Winter 2012): 12, https://journals.sagepub.com/doi/pdf/10.1177/1536504212436479.

30. Dorcas Cheng-Tozun, "What Majority-World Missions Really Looks Like," website of *Christianity Today*, August 26, 2019, https://www.christianitytoday.com/ct/2019/august-web-only/what-majority-world-missions-really-looks-like.html.

31. Zane Pratt, "The Heart of the Task," in *Discovering the Mission of God: Best Missional Practices for the 21st Century*, ed. *Mike Barnett* (Downers Grove, IL: InterVarsity, 2012), 134.

32. Pratt, 131.

33. Dietrich Bonhoeffer, *The Cost of Discipleship* (New York: Touchstone, 1995), 59.

34. J. D. Payne, "Mission and Church Planting," in *Theology and Practice of Mission: God, the Church, and the Nations*, ed. Bruce Riley Ashford (Nashville: B&H, 2011), 209–10.

35. Thomas Hale and Gene Daniels, *On Being a Missionary* (Pasadena, CA: William Carey, 2012), 7.

36. This list of ways to live sent is a combination of missional rhythms from my own experience and the e-book from Verge Network, *Simple Ways to Be Missional*, https://my.vergenetwork.org/simple-ways-to-be-missional-ebook/.

37. Josh Reeves, "25 Simple Ways to Be Missional in Your Neighborhood," Verge Network, December 16, 2014, https://www.vergenetwork.org/2011/08/23/25-simple-ways-to-be-missional-in-your-neighborhood/.

38. The Gospel Map was created by Luke Skeen, with help from Mike S., for Sojourn Church Midtown in Louisville, Kentucky. It has been adapted and used with permission.

39. Moreau, Corwin, and McGee, *Introducing World Missions*, 253.

40. Craig Storti, *Art of Crossing Cultures* (Yarmouth, ME: Intercultural Press, 2001), 67–68.

41. Hale, *On Being a Missionary*, 109.

42. Hale, 98.

43. Jason Mandryk, *Operation World* (Downers Grove, IL: InterVarsity, 2010), 832.

44. This information was presented in a lecture in 2021. Because of security concerns, details of the lecture are not public. For more about the Silas Project, see http://fot-uk.org.uk/the-silas-project/.

45. Max Roser, Hannah Ritchie, and Esteban Ortiz-Ospina, "World Population Growth," Our World in Data, last updated May 2019, https://ourworldindata.org/world-population-growth.

46. The population of Russia is about 144 million according to the World Bank "Population, Total," World Bank website, last revised 2019, https://data.worldbank.org/indicator/sp.pop.totl.

47. "660 Million Evangelicals in the World?" Evangelical Focus, February 18, 2020, https://evangelicalfocus.com/print/5119/660-million-evangelicals-in-the-world.

48. "How Many People Groups Are There?" Joshua Project, accessed January 30, 2022, https://joshuaproject.net/resources/articles/how_many_people_groups_are_there.

49. Claude Hickman, "What Is a People Group?" The Traveling Team, January 30, 2015, http://www.thetravelingteam.org/articles/what-is-a-people-group.

50. "Understand," People Groups, accessed October 18, 2019, https://peoplegroups.org/Understand.aspx.

51. "Global Statistics," Joshua Project, accessed January 30, 2022, https://joshuaproject.net/people_groups/statistics.

52. Tim Keller, foreword to *Why Cities Matter: To God, the Culture, and the Church*, by Stephen T. Um and Justin Buzzard (Wheaton, IL: Crossway, 2013), 9.

53. Um and Buzzard, 10.

54. Jason Mandryk, "The State of the Gospel" in *Perspectives on the World Christian Movement: A Reader*, ed. Ralph D. Winter and Steven C. Hawthorne (Pasadena, CA: William Carey, 2013), 362.

55. Mandryk, 363.

56. Paul Borthwick, *Western Christians in Global Mission: What's the Role of the North American Church?* (Downers Grove, IL: InterVarsity, 2012), 17.

57. Borthwick, 17.

58. Mandryk, "The State of the Gospel," 363.

59. Mandryk, 361.

60. *Westminster Shorter Catechism*, Q&A 1.

61. Philip Yancey, "Finding the Will of God: No Magic Formulas," *Christianity Today*, September 16, 1983, 27.

62. Hale, *On Being a Missionary*, 23.

63. Tom Steffen and Lois McKinney Douglas, *Encountering Missionary Life and Work: Preparing for Intercultural Ministry* (Grand Rapids: Baker, 2008), 39.

64. Adapted from Steve Hoke and Bill Taylor, *Send Me! Your Journey to the Nations* (Wheaton, IL: World Evangelical Fellowship Missions Commission, 1999), 76–78.

mission
propelled by God's Grace

Since 1983, Serge has been helping individuals and churches engage in global mission. From short-term trips to long-term missions—we want to see the power of God's grace transform your own life and motivate and sustain you to move into the lives of others—particularly those who do not yet know Jesus. As a cross-denominational, Reformed, sending agency with more than 300 missionaries in 26 countries across 5 continents, we are always looking for people who are ready to take the next step in sharing Christ. Explore the life-changing opportunities for you to grow and serve around the world through:

- **Short-term Teams:** One- to two-week trips oriented around serving overseas ministries while equipping the local church for mission

- **Internships:** Eight-week to nine-month opportunities to learn about missions through serving with our overseas ministry teams

- **Apprenticeships:** Intensive 12–24 month training and ministry opportunities for those discerning their call to cross-cultural ministry

- **Career:** One- to five-year appointments designed to nurture you for a lifetime of ministry

Serge — Grace at the Fray

Visit us online at:
serge.org/mission

newgrowthpress.com